The Ideas Factory

100 adaptable discussion starters to get teens talking

Martin Saunders

Monarch
BOOKS
Oxford, UK & Grand Rapids, Michigan, USA

First published in the UK in 2007 by Monarch Books
(a publishing imprint of Lion Hudson plc),
Wilkinson House, Jordan Hill Road, Oxford OX2 8DR.
Tel: +44 (0)1865 302750   Fax: +44 (0)1865 302757
Email: monarch@lionhudson.com
 www.lionhudson.com

Cover design: Todd Oliver (www.toli.co.uk)

ISBN: 978-1-85424-834-3 (UK)
ISBN: 978-0-8254-6173-6 (USA)

Distributed by:
UK: Marston Book Services Ltd, PO Box 269, Abingdon, Oxon OX14 4YN;
USA: Kregel Publications, PO Box 2607, Grand Rapids, Michigan 49501.

British Library Cataloguing Data
A catalogue record for this book is available from the British Library.

Printed and bound in Malta by Gutenberg Press.

Contents

Acknowledgments 7

Introduction 9

SECTION A: **True Stories** 18
A1	Racism	20
A2	Emotion	22
A3	Generosity	24
A4	Hope	26
A5	Near-death experience	30
A6	Adultery	32
A7	National rivalry	34
A8	Internet pornography	36
A9	Disaster	38
A10	Perfect partners	40
A11	Courage and conviction	42
A12	Virginity	44
A13	Forgiveness	46
A14	Revenge	50
A15	Political protests	52
A16	Youth	54
A17	Authority	56
A18	Hypocrisy	58
A19	Fashion	60
A20	Reputation	62
A21	Possessions	64
A22	Drugs	66
A23	Advertising	68

| A24 | Rules | 70 |
| A25 | Graffiti | 72 |

SECTION B: **Teen Issues** 74

B1	Music piracy	76
B2	Laziness	78
B3	Unrequited love	82
B4	The Sabbath	84
B5	Pornography	86
B6	Parents	90
B7	Talents and abilities	92
B8	Integrity	96
B9	Sexual guilt	98
B10	Peer pressure/drugs	102
B11	Rejection of homosexuals	104
B12	Stealing	108
B13	Acceptance	110
B14	Cheating	114
B15	Television	118
B16	Healthy relationships... good break-ups	122
B17	The Holy Spirit	124
B18	Jealousy	126
B19	Dieting	130
B20	Violent video games	132
B21	Divorce	134
B22	Eating disorders	136
B23	Fairness	138
B24	Lies and gossip	142
B25	Friendship	144

SECTION C: **Famous Names** 148

    C1   Marriage 150

    C2   Growing up fast 152

    C3   God's deal 154

    C4   Prayer/staying in touch 156

    C5   God's plan 158

    C6   Changing direction 162

    C7   Racism 164

    C8   Friendship 166

    C9   Self-image 168

    C10   Defining moments 170

    C11   Charity 172

    C12   Acting justly 174

    C13   Generosity 176

    C14   Second chances 178

    C15   Imposed religion 180

    C16   Power 182

    C17   Ethics 186

    C18   Giving thanks 188

    C19   Equality 190

    C20   Capital punishment 192

    C21   Perseverance 196

    C22   Atheism 200

    C23   Death 204

    C24   The poor 206

    C25   Names 208

SECTION D: **The Bible in 25 Steps** 210

    D1   Creation (and evolution) 212

    D2   Sin (and suffering) 216

D3	God's people	220
D4	God hears the cry	224
D5	The law (and rules)	228
D6	God's supreme power	232
D7	Israel's greatest king	236
D8	God speaks through his prophets	240
D9	Power	244
D10	Faith in suffering	248
D11	Worship	252
D12	Wisdom (and guidance)	256
D13	A coming Messiah (hope)	260
D14	Renewal (and life balance)	264
D15	Punishment and restoration	268
D16	God sends his son	272
D17	Jesus' line	276
D18	Discipleship	278
D19	Prayer (and forgiveness)	282
D20	Healing	286
D21	Jesus' death and resurrection	288
D22	The Holy Spirit	292
D23	Church	296
D24	Paul	300
D25	Life after death	304
Index		307

Acknowledgments

I'd like to thank the many people who've contributed to this book in various ways: the whole team at *Youthwork* magazine; the readers who sent in story ideas; every poor young person who I've tested these ideas out on over the past few years; my wife Jo for letting me hide in the shed and write; Andy Peck, my on-tap theological heavyweight; Steve Adams, who taught me how to write resources; Grace Benson, who can do pretty much anything; and John Buckeridge, who very foolishly gave me a shot at a job that I was in no way qualified to do.

Introduction

Story is not only our most prolific art form but rivals all activities – work, play eating, exercise – for our waking hours. We tell and take in stories as much as we sleep – and even then we dream. Why? Why is so much of our life spent inside stories? Because, as critic Kenneth Burke tells us, stories are equipment for living.   Robert McKee, *Story* (Methuen, 1999)

The power of story

The teenage appetite for story remains unquenchable. If anything, with the advent of new technologies offering greater choice of stories than ever before, that appetite has grown. Today's teens may not spend half of their lives in the library (although some do), but in a range of other places – some real, some virtual – they greedily guzzle on story, day and night. Television, cinema, the Internet, podcasts, video games – all play host to a constant stream of narratives for young people to absorb.

They're not just consumers in this, however; young people are also story-tellers. Often, they're great story-tellers. Any suburban train or bus journey around school turn-out time will give you the proof of this. Young people love to regurgitate the stories they've heard – true, fictional and those which fit between the two. They also like to recommend stories to one another – youth culture's way of circumventing the marketing man. So many teenage conversations, in my experience, seem to begin with 'Have you seen...?' or 'Have you played...?'

Play is an increasing mechanism through which young people are consuming story. Since the 1980s, the video-game industry has steadily grown, capturing the imaginations of generations of young people along the way. Back in 1984 – when my tech-obsessed father brought home our first primitive computer – the games and their storylines were simplistic, to say the least. One leading title for the ZX Spectrum was called *Horace Goes Skiing*. You didn't even need to load it up to know exactly what the story was going to be.

Fast forward more than two decades, and the technology has moved on more than anyone in the industry could have predicted. Driven by a desperate ongoing battle for the market between the gaming giants Sony, Atari, Sega, Nintendo and Microsoft, video games have become hyper-real, totally immersive, and packed with the kind of artificial intelligence that would have made *2001*'s HAL blush. Graphic images border on the photographic; surround-sound is standard; and a comparable investment has been made in storyline. For a while now, games have even had their own scriptwriters.

The lines between Hollywood and the gaming industry have now become so blurred that a fascinating two-way synergy is now taking place. In recent years, Hollywood has churned out a series of movies based on games, including two *Resident Evil*s, *Doom*, *Silent Hill*, *Bloodrayne* and *House of the Dead*. All have been one-star awful without exception, and interestingly, all are based on games from the 'survival–horror' genre. In the other direction, many video games are now developed in parallel with their corresponding movies. Big-name actors provide the voices for their virtual counterparts – as was the case with Electronic Arts' popular series of *Lord of the Rings* games. When the Wachowski brothers made the much-maligned Matrix sequels, they filmed so much extra content that the stars were often unaware whether the scene they were filming would appear in a game or a film.

So the way we tell stories is changing, but story still forms the beating heart of our culture. This book is designed to help you engage with that – to tap into the imaginations and cultural databanks in young people's heads, and to unleash their ability to tell, process and discuss stories.

Uncommunicative community

While early-third-millennium young people might be communicating more, it seems they're talking less. The digital generation are finding new and exciting methods of correspondence all the time, but none of them appear to involve standing toe-to-toe with another human being. Web communities, mobile phones, Xbox Live, email, instant messaging – all offer a way for a young person to meet more people and have far more 'friends' than they could have dreamed of before. Yet while each of these platforms is part of a much heralded communications revolution, the less publicized flipside is that they threaten to create a communication blackout. Today's teenagers – and pre-teens, and young adults, and pretty much any other demographic group – now have the opportunity to retreat into a digital shell, where face-to-face conversation is far from compulsory. All the risks of classic human interaction – tension, argument, passion – are stripped away. The great attraction, beyond the technological bells and whistles, is that conversation is much 'safer' this way.

There are the more severe cases, of course – principally those young people who are bullied, depressed, or suffer from low self-esteem. Yet this cultural shift is impacting far more widely than those individuals, and is touching an entire generation. While the right-wing press might worry over the way text messaging is ruining yng ppls ablty 2 spll, there are far greater dangers for them to get themselves worked into a fluster about. Never mind their capacity to spell the Queen's English – what about their ability to speak it?

In decades past, young people had two options if they wanted to talk to one another outside of normal social hours. The telephone offered the most obvious alternative; and as a last resort, they might even have written a letter. But both of these methods contributed to building up an existing relationship, and helped to strengthen and consolidate it. Many of the newer forms of communications technology allow young people to make completely new 'buddies' in far-off parts of the world. They can hide behind aliases and avatars, and they may not even know one another's real names. And while they type, and 'post' and 'nudge', very often, they don't hear one another's voices. They don't talk to each other.

If Christian youth workers are really passionate about helping young people to grow into well-rounded young adults, then this area should be of real interest. Not because they're worried about slipping literacy standards, but because the ability to hold a conversation has been a well-proven bedrock of civilization for thousands of years. Or rather, conversation is the bedrock of community, and communities are the building-blocks of civilization.

Whatever the marketing men might tell us, virtual communities can't take the place of physical communities. They might appear to involve less personal investment and risk (although, sadly, we know that isn't true), but they're ultimately hollow and dishonest. No one reveals their true self online, for the simple reason that one doesn't have to. In an Internet discussion, you can pretend to be whoever you want. Virtual communities are all about hiding behind an edited version of yourself – your looks, your achievements, your abilities – that you choose to present to the world. They're the polar opposite of genuine communities, which are about truth; about stripping away the pretence and baring your soul. In a virtual community, you're supposed to lie; after all, who would choose to reveal their flaws if no one could see them?

What does this then foster in the lives of the young people who choose the virtual life above traditional friendship communities? Not only are they denied the environment in which social skills are learned and honed, but they are also inhabiting a virtual social world in which dishonesty and untruth are key features of the landscape.

Even putting this uncomfortable reality aside, Christians have another especially good reason to defend the traditional notion of relationship community: it is a construct that was made by God himself. Right at the start, when God made Adam, he immediately asserted that 'it is not good for the man to be alone' (Genesis 2:18), and promptly created Eve as a companion. This is the same God who, even before creation, lived in community in his own Holy Trinity (see Genesis 1:2; John 1:1–2). The Bible does not advocate a life lived in isolation.

It's important to make clear that not all of Britain's young people are currently checking out of the real world and moving into the digital ghetto. We're not even talking about a majority. Most young people enjoy healthy physical community with real friends who they know inside out. Beyond this, it's also true to say that the majority of young people who choose to embrace this technological revolution – with their Xbox Live headsets, prosthetically-attached mobile phones and Facebook friend lists always on standby – still retain the ability and desire to function in the real world, learning three-dimensional social skills along the way. But a significant minority do not. What we are seeing at present is a less-than-gentle erosion of a youth culture that has face-to-face conversation at its heart.

It's perhaps ironic that British Telecom, at the forefront of the broad-band roll-out that has facilitated this communications revolution, once used as its tagline the phrase 'It's good to talk.' Now, more and more young people are voting with their mouse-pointers and near-arthritic texting thumbs that, like the advertising campaign which accompanied it, that notion has become a thing of the past.

All of which is very bad news for the youth worker. In an article in *Youthwork* magazine in May 2006, the youth ministry lecturer and practitioner Arthur Brown identified conversation as *the* key element of all youth work:

Going back to the question of 'what it is we do' as youth workers, when was the last time you heard someone answer, 'we talk'? Often people say that youth work is about building relationships. But how does this happen? Through talking. People say that youth work and ministry is about teaching. How best do most of us learn? Through talking... sharing ideas with others, allowing the opinions of others to enter our own thought processes. This is especially important for young people as they explore their own identity, values and beliefs.

Talk is our bread and butter. It's our equivalent of the surgeon's scalpel or the footballer's boots. It's the key tool with which all of us – voluntary or full-time, faith-based or statutory-based – do our job. We talk; yet if the present trend towards virtual community continues or, as expected, accelerates beyond our imagination, we may be left working with a generation of young people who don't want to talk – or don't know how. We could be left talking to ourselves.

So the idea of 'getting young people talking' – the need which this book claims to help you meet – is a solid and urgent one.

The big story

As Christians, we have one particular story that we're excited about, and it's a story which we want to get young people talking about. The Bible is often referred to as God's handbook for life, but that shouldn't lead us to believe that it belongs on the shelf next to a car service manual and a recipe book.

One of the great joys of reading the Bible from cover to cover is the realization you experience, that as well as being the Word of God, it's also a very fine piece of literature. We shouldn't ever feel embarrassed about the Bible in terms of its appeal to young people. The stories within it (and the over-arching narrative) are more than powerful enough to grip a young person. As Rob Bell says, 'I have faith in the text.'

This book is intended to help you to connect God's big story with young people's inbuilt sense of story, and so every single one of the 100 resources within it hooks the discussion into a Bible passage. As I was writing, however, I became convinced not only of the need to hook young people into Bible stories, but also of the great worth of helping them to see what's going on in the whole Bible. It's a daunting and massive book, but if we're not equipped to see it as a whole story, and only focus on the thousands of smaller stories that make it up, we can miss a lot of what's really going on. The story of Moses bringing the Israelites out of Egypt means so much more in the context of the fall and the coming of Jesus, for instance. If we can teach young people how it all fits together, I believe their story-sensors will go into overdrive. When you're able to pull back and see the wood and not just the trees, it's an astounding view. For this reason, the last part of the book aims to help you do exactly that.

The discussion starters

These 100 discussion starters are intended to help you to get young people talking, to engage their sense of story, and to point them towards the bigger story that's not just confined to a book, but going on all around them. Each discussion starter is presented in four fairly uniform steps: a discussion trigger, and three banks of questions.

The **Discussion trigger** is a short story or introduction, which you can either read to your young people, give to them to read, or both. There is huge variety in these; they're intended as a tin-opener and little more, and don't go into great detail. You may wish to add some words of your own to flesh them out, but I have deliberately made them brief, as experience tells me that while young people like to hear a story, they don't particularly want a three-point sermon. Each discussion trigger opens up at least one theme, which is then unpacked in the questions below it.

The **Opening up** questions are designed to spark the discussion into life. They are generally lower in impact, although you may still see the conversation catch fire! These questions are not always of a spiritual nature, and are more likely to refer to the story in the discussion trigger.

The **Digging deeper** questions tie more directly to the main theme, and are not (apart from in the last section of the book) aimed specifically at Christians. No assumptions are made about faith; these questions are designed as a tool for you to use in guiding and facilitating conversations. You may wish to provide your own answers to these, pointing more directly at the Christian perspective, but they do not explicitly reference spiritual themes.

The **Taking it to the Word** bank of questions is a Bible study, mainly aimed at Christian groups, or young people who are interested in exploring Christianity. They are not intended for use with young people who have made no such suggestion. It is important to note that not all of these question banks leave the group with a nice, neat conclusion – it's up to the group facilitator to draw things to a close as he or she sees fit.

The book is divided into four Sections, each containing twenty-five discussion starters: The Sections are:

- 'True Stories': real events from the news that make a real point.
- 'Teen Issues': semi-fictional stories, many of which are based on real events. Names have been changed to protect the innocent and the guilty!
- 'Famous Names': what celebrities, public figures and other famous people have done in the media spotlight.

- 'The Bible in 25 Steps': an overview of the key events in the Bible, and how they all fit together. This last set of discussion guides is slightly different in style, and is aimed specifically at Christian young people.

Adapting and other preparation

This book is intended as a resource, but I strongly recommend that you do not view it simply as a get-out-of-jail-free card, to be pulled out at the last minute and used as is. To get the most out of the discussion guides, and to really make them work for your group, I suggest you take some time ahead of your meeting to adapt them to your context. This might mean slightly changing the wording, or adding or removing questions.

If you're working with unchurched young people, for instance, you may wish to delete the 'Taking it to the Word' questions completely, or reduce their number. If you have a longer session, you may wish to add your own questions in the 'Digging deeper' section. Think hard about your audience, and which areas of the discussion you feel will help or interest them most. I also advise that you treat subjects such as family, self-image and sexuality with extra caution, and try to anticipate any questions which might create an uncomfortable or upsetting situation for some of your young people.

To aid your efforts in presenting the meetings, this book includes a licence to photocopy for the person who bought it. Some young people will find it much easier to consider questions if they can read, rather than listen to them. Respectfully, I ask that you don't share this material beyond your own group and work, for obvious reasons.

That's it. I hope this resource is genuinely helpful as you seek to get young people talking about the important stuff. Encourage them to open up, expect the unexpected, and above all, have fun!

Section A
True Stories

Introduction

We live in strange times. The media, which is everywhere, offers a constant stream of weirdness across television channels, magazines and websites, and those stories are picked up and distributed by their startled consumers. The stranger the story, the more inclined we are to retell it, and so around the water-coolers, common-rooms, bars and coffee-shops of our society, we pass these nuggets of strangeness on, over and over again. Often they involve misfortune and pain – even death; sometimes they involve an unlikely choice or an error of judgment. One thing links them all though, and it's the thing that attracts us: these are the stories of real people, doing really strange things, in the real world.

Whether it's 'Rock Star Ate My Hamster' or 'Man Eaten by Collapsible Bed', they're always the stories that our eyes are drawn to first. They may be far less worthy than current affairs and world politics, but boy, are they more entertaining.

And that's as far as these stories usually go. A quick laugh, or grimace, or a combination of both, and then we pass the tale on and forget about it. How many times have you forwarded on a bizarre viral email about a man stuck in a lift or a woman who eats live snakes, and then forgotten about it? The media allow us to briefly skirt past these interesting lives as if we're on some kind of gigantic museum tour, and then we forget them just as quickly. For the people involved, it could be the defining moment of their lives. For us, it's just one more stop on the voyeuristic media journey.

Over the next few pages, you'll find twenty-five discussion starters based around exactly these kinds of stories. There's a woman who falls into a coma whenever she feels strong emotion; a German prince with a castle but no princess to love; and a young film-maker who died of a drug overdose after making an anti-drugs video. As you read the stories, you'll probably find at least some that startle you into telling a friend.

The aim here, though, is to take these stories one step further. As you read them, ask yourself: What do they tell you about the world around you? How can they help us to understand life in the twenty-first century? Each story comes with a range of questions to help you and your group to do just that. Feel free to add your own.

In addition, each story is linked to a Bible passage which covers a similar theme. These passages are designed to help you to explore what God thinks about the issue involved; to decode the story in the light of his Word; even to look for his presence within the story.

Christianity is a real faith, about a real God who operates in the real world. Taking the time to look more closely at the realities of that world can help young people to understand his relevance, and that of his Word, in the strange times that we live in.

A1

THEME: **Racism**

BIBLE: **Acts 10**

The Nazi pop twins

With their perfect blue eyes and long blonde hair, the 15-year-old Gaede sisters appear at first glance to be clones of the worryingly successful Olsen twins. But the hair and the eyes are all part of the far more terrifying truth about the pretty Californian teens and their pop band, Prussian Blue – they've become flag-bearers for the American neo-Nazi movement.

Clad in smiley-Hitler T-shirts, twins Lamb and Lynx Gaede lead crowds in *Sieg Heil* salutes at concerts and Holocaust-denial festivals. The girls' White Supremacist fan-base goes wild for tracks such as 'Sacrifice', which eulogizes Hitler's deputy Rudolph Hess, and *'Weiss, Weiss, Weiss'*, which translates from German as 'White, White, White'. Driven by their White Nationalist parents, the girls recently came under fire for insisting that their donation to the Hurricane Katrina relief fund should go only to help white people.

'We think our race is different to other races in positive ways and that we've done more for civilization,' says Lynx. 'We don't want to harm other races, but we don't have to take care of them or be around them.'

OPENING UP

➤ Were you aware that this kind of belief existed? How does this story make you feel or react?

➤ What are your beliefs about racism in this country? What is racism? Is it present in your community any more? If so, how?

➤ How do you believe Lamb and Lynx have arrived at this set of beliefs? What is your view of the girls?

DIGGING DEEPER

➤ Take a moment on your own in silence, to explore your own prejudices. Be really honest – what are you prejudiced about? Who don't you treat equally?

➤ What do you think is the worst kind of prejudice? Why?

➤ Discuss with others – where do you see different kinds of prejudice in your local community? What could you practically do to change these situations?

➤ What might the world be like if we did as the girls suggest, and live in segregation? How would the people involved feel? How might the world change?

TAKING IT TO THE WORD

➤ **Read** Acts 10: 9–35.

➤ What did Peter believe about other races? How was he wrong?

➤ What do these verses tell us about prejudice as a whole? If we're honest, do we make the same kinds of errors, consciously and unconsciously? Do you think you/your church/ your group live out this story?

➤ Write out verses 34–35 on a sheet of paper – make this your group's value statement on racism and prejudice. Pray together that in following in God's footsteps, you might live this out in practice.

A2

THEME: **Emotion**

BIBLE: **2 Samuel 6**

Emotions on hold

Many people find it difficult to show their emotions, but for one woman, to do so puts her health at risk. Wendy Richmond, aged 53, suffers from a rare condition which places her in a coma whenever she becomes emotional or wants to laugh or cry. Her illness means that she has to remain emotionally reserved at all times, steer clear of sad movies and humorous television programmes, and even refrain from saying 'I love you' to her family.

Mrs Richmond suffers from a rare mix of sleep-related illnesses, and although treatment is available, it's expensive and her local healthcare trust refuses to pay the annual £9,000 bill to treat her. As a result, she is left to cope with a condition which she says has left her with several failed relationships.

Things became particularly difficult with the birth of Mrs Richmond's first granddaughter Megan. Mrs Richmond recently told a newspaper: 'I want to sweep her up into my arms and say, "I love you". But I am afraid it could be dangerous for both of us. It could trigger an episode and I could collapse on the floor, injuring Megan and myself. It is quite bizarre to think that I can't tell my family I love them without falling over.'

OPENING UP

➤ What is your initial response to this story? How does it make you feel?

➤ Do you find it easy or difficult to show your emotions? Explain your answer.

➤ Do you take your ability to laugh or cry for granted? What does this story teach us?

DIGGING DEEPER

➤ Do you have friends or family members who find it particularly easy or difficult to show emotion? How do you feel when you're around them?

➤ Are you more of a 'thinker' or a 'feeler'? Which would you rather be?

➤ Why are emotions important? How might your life be easier or more difficult without them?

TAKING IT TO THE WORD

➤ **Read** 2 Samuel 6:1–16.

➤ The great leader David is angry (verse 8), fearful (verse 9) and joyful (verse 14) within the space of a few verses. What does this tell us about him?

➤ David dances wildly even though he is a king. How do you feel about this?

➤ What do you make of the response of David's wife, Michal?

➤ Are you more like David or Michal when it comes to displaying emotion before God? What about in front of friends or family?

A3

THEME: **Generosity**

BIBLE: **2 Corinthians 8 – 9**

The cheerful giver

An 83-year-old lottery winner was heralded as Britain's most generous man, after giving away his entire £3.5 million fortune in just two months. Bob Bradley, from Llanelli, made large donations to children's charities, and spent the rest on presents for his family and friends. The gifts ranged from a £500,000 home, bought for his grandson, to a pet rabbit for his great-grand-daughter, which cost £8.50. He also bought a £70,000 Mercedes for his son, and a nail salon for his grand-son's wife.

War veteran Mr Bradley, who took part in the D-Day landings, scooped £3,570,000 on his 83rd birthday. 'I want nothing for myself,' he told reporters, 'but every-thing for my family. I want to make sure their dreams come true.' Mr Bradley said that the joy he received from watching his family enjoy themselves was a big enough reward for him. 'I already feel like I had won the jackpot before it happened,' he said. 'I had got good health and a wonderful family. No amount of money can buy that.'

OPENING UP

➤ What would you do with £3.5 million? Would you give it all away?

➤ What do you make of Bob Bradley's use of the money? Why do you think he did it? What do you think most people would think about this story?

➤ What might the long-term consequences of Mr Bradley's generosity be?

DIGGING DEEPER

➤ How generous are you, on a scale of 1 to 10? How do you compare to: your friends? Your family? Mr Bradley?

➤ If you were a contestant on a quiz show where the money had to be given to charity, who would you give it to, and why?

➤ Do you think it would be easier to give away half of: £1,000, £10,000 or £1 million? Explain your answer.

TAKING IT TO THE WORD

➤ **Read** 2 Corinthians 8:1–15 and 9:6–8.

➤ What do you learn from this passage about what was going on in the Macedonian church?

➤ How does Paul describe their generosity? What else does he say about it?

➤ Why is giving important for Christians? What other passages back this up?

➤ In the second reading, what does it mean to reap and sow generously, and to be 'a cheerful giver'? How does this link with the story above?

A4
THEME: **Hope**
BIBLE: **Jeremiah 29**

When all hope is lost...

If you realized that the plane you were on was about to crash into a remote mountain, you could perhaps be forgiven for losing all hope of survival. And if you did then survive, only to learn that the search for you and the other survivors had been abandoned, how difficult might it be to keep believing that you'd ever see your family and friends again?

This was exactly the nightmare faced by a Uruguayan man named Nando Parrado, when the flight carrying his rugby team crashed in the frozen Andes. One of a handful of crash survivors, he awoke from a coma days later to hear a radio broadcast revealing that the search parties had given up. Yet Nando did not share their lack of faith. Summoning up superhuman strength and perseverance, and focusing on unswerving hope, Nando and his two fellow survivors began a gruelling trek across the mountains towards their eventual rescuers. Along the way, they were forced to eat the flesh of their dead team-mates to avoid starvation, and Nando today describes the experience as 'a living hell'. Even allowing for the harshest interpretations of that word, it's hard to disagree.

Despite his seemingly hopeless plight, Nando did survive the crash, the coma, and the treacherous journey, and in the thirty-six years that have passed, he has enjoyed a more full and varied life than most people dream of – including careers as a racing driver, a television presenter and an author. Even in the most impossible situations, his story is proof positive that hope is never truly lost.

OPENING UP

➤ Put yourself in Nando's position as he wakes among the plane wreckage. How do you think you would cope? How much hope do you think you'd have?

➤ What do you think Nando's hope was placed in? His own ability to survive? God? Or something else?

➤ How might surviving an ordeal like this change your perspective on life?

➤ What to you is the difference between hope and faith?

DIGGING DEEPER

➤ What do you hope for?

➤ What kinds of things do people in our society hope for today? Think about different areas of life – relationships, career, sport, the future.

➤ What are the advantages and disadvantages of these kinds of hope?

TAKING IT TO THE WORD

➤ **Read** Jeremiah 29:11–14.

      ➤ How do these verses give Christians hope?

      ➤ What does God require from us here?

      ➤ Would these verses help you in a situation like the one faced by Nando? Why or why not?

      ➤ How are hope and prayer linked?

A5

THEME: **Near-death experience**

BIBLE: **Psalm 55 and Luke 12**

Last minute not gone

Daniel Cave is regarded among his friends as the luckiest man alive. Not because he has a big house, a great job, or a beautiful wife, but because he stared death in the face, and walked away. But Daniel, a Christian from Seattle, doesn't agree with his friends. He doesn't think luck had anything to do with it.

Since he was 12 years old, Daniel had always dreamed of skydiving. But it wasn't until after his 26th birthday that he eventually plucked up the courage to try it. In hindsight, he may wish he'd chosen to play golf instead. For as he descended from 1,100 feet at trouser-ruining speed, Daniel realized that he'd picked up a dodgy parachute. No matter how hard he tugged, it wouldn't open.

With seemingly seconds to live, this human lead balloon uttered a few words of prayer: 'OK, God. Well, I trust you, I believe in you, and if there's any way, I'd love to see my family again, so help me out here.' Daniel hit the ground seconds later, and lived – a feat that doctors later called 'impossible'.

OPENING UP

➤ Why do you believe Daniel Cave survived?

➤ If you were falling to the ground from 1,100 feet, what would you do in your likely last moments?

➤ Why do you think people who have no faith often choose to pray when they're in mortal danger? What else might they do instead?

DIGGING DEEPER

➤ Daniel believes prayer saved him. What other stories have you heard where people have made similar claims?

➤ Have you ever prayed when things were tough? What happened afterwards?

➤ How bad does life have to get for you to start praying? Or do you pray when things are going well?

TAKING IT TO THE WORD

➤ **Read** Psalm 55:16–18 and Luke 12:16–21.

➤ What does this Psalm have to say to us about the bad situations in our lives? What should our response to them be? Do you really believe in this?

➤ If you died tonight, what do you believe would happen to you next?

➤ Most people pray when their plane is about to crash – but what if they don't get the chance? What does Jesus say to people who put God off until tomorrow?

A6
THEME: ## Adultery
BIBLE: ## Proverbs 6

His Fake Alibi

Mr and Mrs Truelove had enjoyed a fairly happy first few years of marriage, but just now, some of the gloss was starting to rub off. Mr Truelove was working longer hours at night, even though none of his colleagues seemed to. At weekends, he would disappear for golf trips which turned into evenings out and then overnight stays. They weren't spending any quality time together any more.

After a few months, Mrs Truelove became suspicious that her husband might be having an affair. She called his office, late one night, and another man answered. She was told that her husband was in the building, but on an important conference call to the US. A few minutes later, her husband called back. It appeared that she had got it all wrong. She felt incredibly guilty.

What Mrs Truelove didn't realize, however, was that her husband was using a service called Fake Alibi, run by a company who are prepared to lie for you. They'll provide fake conference invitations, fake bank statements – even a fake job, so that customers can put together a really authentic lie. Mr Truelove had been having an affair for six months – and thanks to the Alibi service, his wife would probably never find out.

OPENING UP

➤ How do you feel about the existence of this company?

➤ Could it ever be better to use a company like this than to tell the truth? Explain your answer.

➤ What do you think will happen to the Trueloves' marriage in the long term?

DIGGING DEEPER

➤ Why do you think people cheat on one another?

➤ What strategies do you think married couples should put in place to stop themselves from having an affair? What about unmarried couples?

➤ Do you think it's better to have an affair in secret and stay married, or to ask for a divorce and break up a family? Why?

TAKING IT TO THE WORD

➤ **Read** Proverbs 6:20–35.

➤ Why do you think these verses are so harsh?

➤ What strikes you most about this passage? Do you think the consequences described are still paid by adulterers today? Do you think these verses are more or less relevant than they might have been when they were written?

➤ You may not be married, but what do these verses say to you about the way you should conduct any romantic relationships?

A7

THEME: **National rivalry**

BIBLE: **Romans 12**

Two World Wars and one World Cup

Every time England plays in a major football championship, it seems to happen. Though completely random, the 'luck of the draw' will always throw up one of the country's traditional nemeses – Argentina or Germany. In six of the last ten tournaments they've played in, England have faced, and usually lost to, one of their old enemies. It drives supporters mad – especially when it's on penalties!

Ask the average supporter why the rivalries exist, and they'll point to Diego Maradona's handball in the 1986 World Cup, or the penalties defeat by Germany in 1990. Perhaps there's a darker reason, however. Before the England vs. Germany game in Euro 2000, *The Sun*'s front page made direct reference to the Second World War. Meanwhile Maradona recently described his 'hand of God' moment as 'payback for the Falklands' (a war in the 1980s between British and Argentinean forces).

Many football fans hold and pass on racist grudges that began in international conflict. England supporters sing songs to rival fans such as 'Ten German Bombers', even though few of them were even alive to experience the war.

OPENING UP

> ➤ Does it matter more when your national sporting teams play against historic national rivals? Why or why not?

> ➤ Are you a football fanatic? Or is someone close to you? How important is football to you around a World Cup?

> ➤ Why do you think people connect international warfare with soccer?

DIGGING DEEPER

> ➤ Why does sport bring out so much passion, positive and negative?

> ➤ Do you think it's a good thing that people experience such strong emotions around sporting events? Explain your answer.

> ➤ How do the media elevate the passions and rivalries around sports?

> ➤ Do you see any similarities between sport and religion? Explain.

TAKING IT TO THE WORD

➤ **Read** Romans 12:9–19.

> ➤ Paul describes the kind of love-centred lifestyle that we should aspire to. How could football fanaticism compromise that lifestyle?

> ➤ What do these verses (especially 18–19) say about grudges?

> ➤ How might you live differently to your peers in the light of these verses, especially during the World Cup?

A8

THEME: # Internet pornography
BIBLE: # Matthew 5

Virtually unfaithful

The people of the Romanian town of Gelati had long admired the strong and lasting marriage of Ana and Florin Pelcu. For twenty-three years they'd lived together in wedded bliss, raising two wonderful children and maintaining a healthy family unit while many relationships in the town faltered. But all that changed one day, when Ana returned home early from work to find Florin with another woman. Well, sort of...

The 'other woman' in question had never kissed Florin. In fact, she'd never even met him. She was a model on an Internet porn site, which Florin had been looking at when his wife unexpectedly returned. Ana was shocked, disgusted and outraged – she felt betrayed by her husband, and immediately asked him to leave. A few days later, she demanded a divorce, saying that she couldn't go on with the marriage because she felt cheated.

A bemused Florin begged his wife to reconsider, claiming that the punishment didn't fit the crime. Ana, however, was insistent, telling a local newspaper: 'What he does is totally away from my principles of life and I don't want to be near him when he does that. I want to set him free so he can find himself the woman he likes.'

OPENING UP

➤ Do you think Ana's decision to divorce her husband was fair? Why or why not?

➤ If you caught a boyfriend or girlfriend looking at pornography, how would you react?

DIGGING DEEPER

➤ Do you think looking at pornography is a big deal? Why?

➤ How widespread do you think pornography use is in your culture?

➤ Why do you think pornography can become so addictive?

➤ What strategies might people be able to put in place to help them stop looking at porn?

TAKING IT TO THE WORD

➤ **Read** Matthew 5:27–30.

➤ What do you think about Jesus' claim here about looking lustfully at a woman? Why do you think he says this?

➤ Jesus didn't operate in the time of the Internet, but in the light of these verses, what do you think about Ana's reaction?

➤ Do you think Jesus is being serious in verses 29–30? What do you think these verses mean?

➤ If lust is an issue for you, and it's appropriate, find a good friend of the same sex, and become accountable to each other on this key issue.

A9

THEME: Disaster

BIBLE: Genesis 3; Romans 8; Psalm 46

Why?

In January 2005, literally millions of people began the long process of grieving for loved ones lost in the Asian Tsunami disaster. In a few horrific moments, huge waves, ten feet high, swept across Indonesia, Sri Lanka, India and elsewhere, bringing death and devastation to unsuspecting people. In the same month, the body of a murdered teenage girl was discovered in England. In the same month, hundreds of Iraqis were killed as the fighting in their country continued. Throughout that month, many people had the same questions on their lips: Why do bad things happen to good people? Why does God allow suffering like this to happen?

OPENING UP

➤ What do you feel when bad things happen to you and those around you?

➤ Being as honest as you can, do news stories like the ones mentioned above make you think about or doubt God?

➤ Consider the following examples of suffering: a gangland shooting; famine in Africa; death from a heart attack. In each case, who or what is ultimately responsible?

DIGGING DEEPER

➤ Name some terrible events that have happened in the world in the past twelve months. Who were the victims? Who was to blame?

➤ What kinds of news stories upset you most? Why?

➤ Why do you think God allows suffering?

TAKING IT TO THE WORD

(Note: There are several banks of questions below – you may wish to select those which you feel are most appropriate.)

➤ **Read** Genesis 3 (especially verses 1–7, 17).

➤ This is the point at which evil entered the world, through sin. What might our lives have been like if 'the fall' had never happened?

➤ What are the consequences of this moment?

➤ All human suffering springs out of the fall. How do you feel about that?

➤ **Read** Romans 8:19–25.

➤ How was creation affected by the fall?

➤ What insight does this give us into the Tsunami disaster? How do you feel about this?

➤ **To finish, read** Psalm 46:1–3.

➤ Very often, stories of tragedy are paired with stories of hope. Can you think of famous examples of this? Can you give examples from your own life or community?

➤ What does this tell us about the way in which God works?

A10

THEME: **Perfect partners**

BIBLE: **Proverbs 31**

An ideal husband

If you were a genuine German prince, with a thirty-bedroom stately home and a personal forest, how would you find your princess? Perhaps you'd employ the same technique as Prince Ruediger of Saxony, who recently took out a 'lonely hearts' advert in a national newspaper.

The 51-year-old prince's advert in the tabloid *Bild* reads: 'Genuine prince, sweet natured and industrious, is seeking after much disappointment a decent woman aged between 25 and 50 for marriage. Pocket money of 2,500 euros a month.' Although the ideal candidate would be a princess from Saxony, the loveless prince is also prepared to settle for a member of the British royal family. Either way, commoners probably need not apply.

There is a catch, though – the prince isn't just looking for a gold-digger who'll spend her days and his millions in the shops. Instead, he wants a girl who'll get her hands dirty assisting in the upkeep of the royal estate. If she'll agree to that, then she'll also enjoy gala balls, beautiful jewellery and plenty of foreign travel.

OPENING UP

➤ Do you think the prince's advert will prove a success?

➤ How do you expect to find your ideal man/woman? (A lot of people don't end up married – this is fine too!)

➤ What would you look for in a wife/husband? Make a list of the most important things to you, and try to place them in order of priority.

DIGGING DEEPER

➤ How do you choose who you'll go out with? What are the factors that have caused you to choose boyfriends/girlfriends in the past?

➤ What have you learned from any relationships you've had with members of the opposite sex – even if you were just friends?

➤ What would be the biggest no-no in a prospective boyfriend or girlfriend? Bad teeth? An annoying laugh? What about personality traits?

TAKING IT TO THE WORD

➤ **Read** Proverbs 31:10–31 in the NCV or Message translations.

➤ This is a biblical description of the perfect partner. Which attributes on this list would you like in a wife or husband?

➤ How does this list differ from the things you wrote on your original wish list?

➤ Pray together, that God will help you to make wise relationship choices.

A11

THEME: **Courage and conviction**

BIBLE: **Jeremiah 26**

The insistent heroine

Like so many other people holidaying in South-East Asia in December 2004, 11-year-old Tilly Smith was not expecting to become caught up in one of the biggest disasters of modern times. However, when she was, her presence of mind saved more than a hundred other tourists from the deadly waves of the infamous tsunami.

Playing on a beach in Phuket, Thailand, Tilly was struck by strange goings-on in the sea. She noticed that the water was bubbling – 'all frothy like the top of a beer'. This occurred to her as odd, before she remembered similar images in a video shown to her in a geography class – a video about how a tsunami forms. Immediately she warned her parents, but they did not believe her.

Tilly was not about to give up – she was sure that danger was not far away. She became hysterical, and eventually, her mum and dad warned other holiday-makers to clear the beach and hotel. Shortly after-wards, the tsunami hit the now empty beach. Around 200,000 people across the region were killed. The tourists from Tilly's beach survived.

OPENING UP

➤ Why do you think Tilly was so insistent? Do you find it hard to believe that she eventually persuaded everyone to clear the beach? Why or why not?

➤ What does Tilly's story say to you about having courage in your convictions?

➤ In what situations have you memorably stuck to your guns, or backed down when perhaps you shouldn't have? What happened? Are there times when it's right to back down?

DIGGING DEEPER

➤ What are the things that you're most convinced of? Make a list if it's helpful. Talk to others. What are they convinced of? As a group, you could produce a list of your 'convictions'. These could range from 'chocolate is better than vanilla' through to 'God exists'.

➤ How far would you go to insist on, or defend, the convictions that you've described?

➤ How do others see your deepest convictions? How do you see the deep convictions of others?

TAKING IT TO THE WORD

➤ **Read** Jeremiah 26:1–16.

➤ What are the similarities with Tilly's story?

➤ Just like Tilly, Jeremiah is insistent in this passage; he doesn't back down. Why do you think this is, and what would the effect have been on the people?

➤ What does this passage teach us about the virtues of perseverance and courage? How might you grow them more in your own life?

➤ Look also at 1 Timothy 4:12. How is the wisdom of this verse exemplified in Tilly, and how could you apply it more to your own life?

A12
THEME: Virginity

BIBLE: 1 Corinthians 6

True beauty waits

Usually, entrants to beauty pageants adopt a 'platform' issue that is allegedly close to their hearts. Saving the rainforests is always a popular choice, as is feeding the poor. But 22-year-old beauty queen Erika Harold had slightly different priorities. She was crowned as 'Miss Illinois' after speaking out on the subject of 'Teenage Sexual Abstinence: Respect Yourself, Protect Yourself'. However, when it came to the big one – the world-renowned Miss America contest – the state pageant officials decided to enter Erika with the less controversial 'teen violence prevention' platform. No one had consulted Miss Harold, it would seem, for she was soon spotted again expressing her views on pre-marital chastity to anyone who would listen. Pageant officials demanded that she only speak on her official issue, but Erika stuck to her guns. She continued to talk openly about sexual abstinence, and was duly crowned Miss America the following October.

OPENING UP

➤ Why do you think Erika Harold chose sexual abstinence as her 'platform' issue?

➤ Teenage sexual promiscuity has risen sharply in the past few decades. Why do you think that is?

➤ By what age are young people expected to lose their virginity? Who places that expectation on them?

➤ Where does the pressure to have sexual relationships come from?

DIGGING DEEPER

➤ What benefits might there be in waiting until marriage to have sex? What advantages might there be in not waiting? What are the disadvantages of each?

➤ How are virgins viewed by our culture? Do you think people respect the Erika Harolds of this world, or laugh at them?

➤ What do you think God's ideal is regarding sex and teenagers? Why?

TAKING IT TO THE WORD

➤ **Read** 1 Corinthians 6:15–20.

➤ Why does sexual purity matter to God?

➤ What do you think it means to 'sin against your own body'?

➤ What do verses 19–20 mean to you? Does this put a different perspective on sex?

A13

THEME: **Forgiveness**

BIBLE: **Matthew 18**

The forgiving father

When policeman Stephen Oake lost his life in a counter-terrorism operation, no one was more devastated than his father. Robin Oake, himself an officer of thirty years' experience, had watched his son rise through the ranks to become a Special Branch Detective Constable. He had seen him build a happy marriage and father three children, becoming a pillar of the local church and community.

Stephen, whose distinguished career had already included the successful capture of two armed robbers, was at the forefront of a counter-terrorist raid which took place after the deadly poison Ricin was discovered in a North London house. Stephen was with officers who were searching a flat in Crumpsall, Manchester, when one of the suspects who had been detained broke free and grabbed a kitchen knife. Stephen was stabbed in the chest, and died in hospital soon afterwards.

In the aftermath of the killing, the media went to Robin Oake for an emotional response. They expected him to speak of his anger, his hatred of the man who'd murdered his son. But instead, as the cameras rolled and the newsmen reeled, he said this: 'I am praying for the perpetrator of this killing and seeking God's forgiveness for him – praying also that he may now seek God himself and find peace and forgiveness with him.' A response almost as shocking as the murder that provoked it.

OPENING UP

➤ What kinds of things do you find it easy to forgive? Why?

➤ Where does the line come where things get more difficult to forgive?

➤ Re-read Robin Oake's media statement. What do you make of these words?

➤ How do you think Robin found the strength to say and mean them?

DIGGING DEEPER

➤ Make a list of 'crimes and wrongs' which people can commit against each other. These can range from telling a lie to murder. Try to put them in order – which are the 'worst', which are the least bad?

➤ Try to agree an order for these wrongs as a group. If you find that you are disagreeing, have a debate about it.

➤ Look at the final list together. Which would you find easy to forgive, which could you forgive over time, and which could you never forgive someone for?

TAKING IT TO THE WORD

➤ **Read** Matthew 18:21–35.

➤ What does this passage tell us about forgiveness?

➤ Why do you think human forgiveness is important?

➤ What might happen if we don't forgive each other?

➤ Try to think of someone who you need to forgive. Pray, asking God for the strength to be able to forgive them.

A14

THEME: **Revenge**

BIBLE: **Matthew 5**

Act of retribution

When two planes collided in mid-air over southern Germany in July 2002, seventy-one people tragically lost their lives. In the aftermath, as fifty-two Russian school-children who'd been on one of the flights were buried, the finger of blame was pointed at Peter Nielsen, the air-traffic controller responsible for the airspace in which the disaster occurred. It was revealed not only that he had been left solely responsible, with his partner taking a break, but also that he had advised one of the pilots to descend when his own on-board collision detection equipment was advising him to climb.

It had been assumed then that the deadly effects of that incident had come to an end, but nearly two years later, in February 2004, they rippled again. A Russian man, overcome with grief at losing his wife, son and daughter in the crash, sought out Nielsen, and murdered him on his own doorstep. After a brief and heated exchange of words, the man stabbed Nielsen, a 36-year-old Danish national, in front of his wife. A week later, while his burial took place, air traffic across Europe was delayed as a mark of respect.

OPENING UP

➤ What did this killing achieve? Was justice done in the end?

➤ How do you think the killer felt afterwards? What about one week, one month, one year later?

➤ This is revenge on a huge scale. When and why in your lives have you felt the desire to take revenge?

➤ In your own head, try to think of one thing about which you are currently angry or disappointed. Who do you blame – and what has been/is/will be your reaction to them? (Don't share this out loud!)

DIGGING DEEPER

➤ What are some of the things that people feel bitterness about?

➤ Do you know of any grudges that people have held for a long time? What about for ten years or more?

➤ How might carrying a grudge around for a long time affect someone?

➤ What alternatives do they have?

TAKING IT TO THE WORD

➤ **Read** Matthew 5:38–45.

➤ Turning the other cheek may seem a little too idealistic when you lose your wife and children. Is it? Why or why not?

➤ Why do you think Jesus prescribes this course of action? What might the effects of following his advice be – on you? On other people involved?

➤ Pray for the situation you thought about earlier, asking God to help you to respond in a Christ-like manner.

A15
THEME: **Political protests**
BIBLE: **John 2**

Right to protest?

When the British government announced that Allied strikes on Iraq had signalled the beginning of war, many people took to the streets in outrage. A public reaction was expected, but some of the participants took the media by surprise. Rallied by the pressure group 'Stop The War Coalition', hundreds of young people abandoned their school classes for the day to appear at the forefront of nationwide protests.

After a day of marches, rallies and canteen occupations co-ordinated by the Internet and text message, opinion on the protest was divided. Some commentators felt that many young people were exploiting the chance for a day off, while others believed that it was good to see usually apathetic young people showing that they cared about an issue.

Although schools refused to condone the behaviour of their pupils, they generally appreciated their strength of feeling against the war, with most of the young protestors escaping punishment for missing lessons. One headteacher commented: 'This wasn't truancy to escape school. This was truancy to make a point.'

OPENING UP

➤ Should young people have the right to walk out of school to protest? Why or why not?

➤ What kinds of risks were these protestors taking?

➤ Would you protest, or would you consider protesting on this issue? Why or why not?

DIGGING DEEPER

➤ What would you protest about? Why?

➤ What do you think are the best ways of getting the government's attention?

➤ Do you think your government listens to you? Why or why not?

➤ How interested are you in the political process? Are you interested in voting?

TAKING IT TO THE WORD

➤ **Read** John 2:12–16.

➤ What are the similarities and differences between Jesus' protest and the anti-war rallies?

➤ Why did Jesus protest? What drove him?

➤ Would Jesus have marched against war in Iraq?

A16

THEME: **Youth**

BIBLE: **1 Timothy 4**

Wonderboy

Every year Stefano, a baker in a small Italian village, would climb the 7,000-foot mountain nearby to fetch firewood. His son, Emmanuel, had often pestered his father to take him along too, but the journey was not without danger, and so Stefano refused. However, once Emmanuel had reached the age of six, he was allowed to join the expedition, on the understanding that he finished his homework first.

It was lucky that he did. At 5,000 feet, Stefano lost his footing, fell heavily, and broke his leg. He had forgotten his mobile phone, and couldn't move, so reluctantly he asked his son to return to the village to get help, accompanied by their Alsatian dog, Kika. Emmanuel refused to take the dog, frightened that his wounded father might be attacked by a wild boar. Instead, he made the treacherous return trek on his own, then led the startled emergency services to the exact spot where his father lay. Newspaper reports worldwide proclaimed the boy a hero, but he simply said, 'I am not a hero. I just wanted to save my Dad.'

OPENING UP

➤ Imagine Emmanuel's journey down the mountain. How suitable do you think it would be for a lone six year old?

➤ Halfway through the story, did you think that there'd be a happy ending? Why or why not?

➤ Was Emmanuel old enough to make that journey?

DIGGING DEEPER

➤ How aware are you of your age? Who makes you feel young or old? What other factors influence this?

➤ How do you feel about age restrictions for the cinema, alcohol, etc.?

➤ Do you feel that there are situations when people look down on you because you are young? If so, share some examples.

➤ Which of your skills and abilities are you most proud of now? What kinds of strengths would you like to develop with age?

➤ How can you best make use of the strengths, skills and abilities which you have already, to make an impact on your friends, school, family or community?

TAKING IT TO THE WORD

➤ **Read** 1 Timothy 4:12.

➤ What does the Bible say here to young people? What are the implications of that?

➤ How old should you be before you can: (a) preach in church; (b) organize events; (c) lead services; (d) lead cell/home groups? Why?

➤ Discuss: are there things you feel you could do for God, but don't because of your age? What are they? Could you do them anyway?

➤ Pray for one another, asking God for opportunities to serve him, regardless of age.

A17

THEME: **Authority**

BIBLE: **Matthew 7**

Believe it or not?

The people of Swaziland had made a hero of the fearless war reporter Phesheay Dube. His live reports from inside battle-ravaged Baghdad had made for powerful radio throughout the second Gulf War, and kept his nation on the edge of their seats. But then Dube was spotted in his home country, just moments after filing another 'live report', and the embarrassing truth was revealed. He'd actually been broadcasting from the inside of a broom cupboard in the country's parliament building.

In his famous book *Mere Christianity*, the great writer C. S. Lewis points out that we only believe in the Norman Conquest, or the Spanish Armada, because we have heard about it 'on authority' from historians. In the same way, listeners to Dube's broadcasts from Iraq believed him because of the authority attributed to the media. In all probability the Norman Conquest did take place, while Dube's courageous adventure in Baghdad did not. But when we learn things 'on authority', how are we to know the difference?

OPENING UP

➤ Read the following list, then explain why you either believe, or don't believe, that each exists or once existed: the Roman Empire, Madonna, Jupiter, Koala bears, the lost city of Atlantis. Feel free to debate with the rest of your group about those items on which there is disagreement.

➤ How confident are you that the last news report which you saw, heard or read was genuine? Why? Do you trust some sources more than others?

➤ Do you think Phesheay Dube's listeners believed his reports were genuine? Why?

DIGGING DEEPER

➤ Who has authority in your local community? What about in your country?

➤ Who do you respect or look up to? Why?

➤ How do you think you'd need to live your own life in order to earn the respect of others? Do you think this is important or desirable?

TAKING IT TO THE WORD

➤ **Read** Matthew 7:28–29.

➤ How do you think 'one who has authority' differed from regular law teachers?

➤ What gave Jesus his authority? What effects did it have?

➤ Why do you believe Matthew's account of what happened? (Or why don't you?)

➤ What differences are there between the authority of Jesus and the Bible, and the authority of the media, or of scientists and historians?

A18
THEME: Hypocrisy
BIBLE: Matthew 7

Hypocrite!

When Eastbourne councillor Frank West got up to speak at a local council meeting, his stirring speech on a potential health hazard received a rapturous reception. His address, questioning the safety of placing mobile-phone masts in the town's built-up areas, was eloquent and impassioned, and roused great support from a council that had already blocked mast-building plans on his advice.

But there was a problem, and it arose from the lips of one of Mr West's opponents. 'Isn't it true,' asked a fellow councillor, 'that you've allowed a mobile-phone booster device to be placed in the grounds of your own garden-centre business, in this very town?'

Unfortunately for Mr West, it was true. Not only that, but the mast in question was located just yards from the area where customers sat and drank coffee. After that, his passionate words seemed to lose a little of their impact.

OPENING UP

➤ Was Frank West wrong to campaign against mobile-phone masts? Why or why not?

➤ How do you think people will now view him, and the issue?

➤ How can we define hypocrisy?

DIGGING DEEPER

➤ What examples of hypocrisy do you see around you? What do they make you think and feel?

➤ Although it's a very negative word, can you think of situations where hypocrisy could be justified?

TAKING IT TO THE WORD

➤ **Read** Matthew 7:1–5.

➤ What does Jesus mean here with all this talk of wood?

➤ Get into pairs, and talk honestly and confidentially, if possible. Think about the people you criticize. In each case, are you right to do so? Why or why not?

➤ What is the plank in your eye? Pray together, asking God to help you remove it, and to steer you away from hypocrisy.

A19
THEME: **Fashion**
BIBLE: **1 Samuel 16**

Fashion victims?

The fashion industry has been telling people 'you are what you wear' for so long that it's hardly a surprise that some people are starting to believe them. After all, as Adolf Hitler once proved, if you repeat a lie often enough, it eventually becomes thought of as the 'truth'...

In May 2006, a Kent shopping centre decided to ban the wearing of hoods and baseball caps on their premises. Apparently, the managers were fed up with teenage 'yobs' – who wore these clothes – terrorizing their customers and shielding their faces from the CCTV cameras. The newspapers went berserk, many of them praising the decision, and calling for further efforts to 'reclaim our streets' from the teenagers.

Of course, every town has its teenage tearaways, and indeed, some of them do behave pretty horribly at times. However, on an average Saturday afternoon, millions of other young people are playing sport, chilling out with friends, pursuing hobbies or just watching TV. Nevertheless, many adults now think young people are all thuggish, binge-drinking louts, with no respect for anyone older than them. And the dreaded hoodie, now banned in several more public places and even being debated in Parliament, is fast becoming cast as the great evil of our generation.

OPENING UP

➤ Are shopping centres right to ban hoodies and caps? Why or why not?

➤ Why do you think hoodies are so popular? Do you wear them?

➤ Some adults now claim to be afraid of young people. How does that make you feel?

➤ How do you feel about the young people in your high street? Why do you think some of them do behave badly?

DIGGING DEEPER

➤ What do you like to wear? Do you wear what you want to wear? If not, why not?

➤ What influences your choice of fashion?

➤ How important are your clothes to you? How would you feel if you had to walk around in a grey suit all the time?

TAKING IT TO THE WORD

➤ **Read** 1 Samuel 16:1–7.

➤ What do you think God feels about fashion?

➤ What does it mean to look at someone's heart?

➤ If God looked at your heart, what do you think he would see?

A20
THEME: **Reputation**
BIBLE: **Titus 2**

Named and shamed

How would you feel if your bad reputation went before you wherever you went? That was the situation facing three young men in Salford who, due to their involvement with gangs, found their faces plastered all across their local estate.

Each of the teenagers had been handed Anti-Social Behaviour Orders (ABSOs), meaning that any further criminal activity could land them up to five years in jail. Breaches of such orders are common, however, so the council decided to make use of local residents to make sure they didn't offend again. Leaflets and posters were widely distributed across the Brookhouse estate in Eccles, where the youths' previous anti-social behaviour had taken place, to publicize the ABSOs. Local citizens were encouraged to inform the authorities if they spotted the faces in the photographs on the estate.

The move was backed by the Home Office, who denied that this was an attempt to 'name and shame' offenders. Instead, a spokesman insisted that 'the effectiveness of an ABSO depends on the larger community knowing the details.'

OPENING UP

➤ Do you think that the posters are a good or bad idea? Why?

➤ Try to put yourself in the place of one of the young men on the poster. How do you think you'd feel if your reputation went before you, everywhere you went?

➤ What do you think about Anti-Social Behaviour Orders? Do they work? Why or why not?

➤ How would you feel if you received an ASBO?

DIGGING DEEPER

➤ What kind of reputation would you like to have?

➤ How do we gain a good or bad reputation?

➤ Who do you know who has a really good reputation? Describe it – why are they so well regarded?

➤ Can you think of someone famous who has a really bad reputation? Why do they have this?

TAKING IT TO THE WORD

➤ **Read** Titus 2: 6–8 through *twice*.

➤ How does Paul instruct Titus to behave and why?

➤ If we followed the same instructions, what would happen to our reputation among other people?

➤ What are the results when other people see Christians behaving in this way? Ask God to help you to behave in a way that will gain you a good reputation.

A21
THEME: **Possessions**
BIBLE: **Ecclesiastes 5**

Attic of the clones

It was a blow so devastating that the Death Star itself could have delivered it. And unfortunately, the Force was not strong enough in *Star Wars* nut Graham Duck to prevent a lightning strike from destroying his massive collection of Jedi-related toys and memorabilia. Mr Duck was out at a Fathers' Day meal when a lightning bolt struck his roof, causing a fire in the loft where he housed his £25,000 collection. It took the local fire brigade in Cleveland ninety minutes to put out the Ewok-fuelled inferno, by which time the entire collection had been charred like Anakin Skywalker.

No real people were injured in the blaze, although a large Yoda doll needed treatment for first-degree burns. Seven rooms were damaged by smoke, causing around £40,000 worth of damage. However, despite the widespread destruction, Mr Duck was clear about what had upset him most. The 41-year-old told the media that although he was insured for the damage, his smouldering collection of books, toys and rare items was 'priceless' and 'irreplaceable'.

OPENING UP

➤ How do you respond to this story – is it funny, sad, or something else?

➤ Why do you think Mr Duck amassed a £25,000 collection of *Star Wars* toys?

➤ Do you have a collection that you're proud of? Could you give it up? How important is it to you?

DIGGING DEEPER

➤ If you had to pack one suitcase tonight with possessions apart from clothes, what would you take? Discuss your list with a partner.

➤ If you could only take one item away with you, what would it be and why?

➤ How important are your possessions to you? What attitude do you have to material goods? Are you a hoarder, or do you buy little?

TAKING IT TO THE WORD

➤ **Read** Ecclesiastes 5:10–15.

➤ What does this passage tell us about material possessions? Do you agree with what it says, particularly in verse 15?

➤ Look at verse 11. What does this warning say to you? Does it have implications for your life?

➤ Spend some time quietly contemplating your own material wealth. Is there an unhealthy obsession you need to deal with? If so, pray, asking God to help you work through it.

A22
THEME:　**Drugs**

BIBLE:　**James 2**

Practise what you preach

When 15-year-old Ben Hennessy made a short film about the dangers of drug abuse, he didn't realize the tragically prophetic nature of his work. With the help of friends, Ben wrote and directed a short film called *Mixing It* – a cautionary tale about a young man who collapses and dies after taking two different types of drug. The short was made as part of a government-funded project, and received its first screening at Ben's local multiplex, as friends and family watched with pride.

Just a few days after the screening, Ben was dead. Paramedics found him in the garden of his grandparents' home, sweating and shouting incomprehensibly. He was taken to hospital by ambulance, and later died, after his body temperature rose to a staggering 42°C. In the ensuing investigation, his distraught friends admitted that he had taken up to four and a half ecstasy tablets. A toxicologist later revealed evidence that Ben had also been smoking cannabis. Just as his own film had warned, he had paid the terrible price of taking and mixing drugs.

OPENING UP

➤ What are your views on drugs? What are the views of some of your non-Christian friends and peers?

➤ Do you think you receive enough education about drugs? What would this look like?

➤ Why do you think Ben Hennessy was able to ignore the warnings of his own film?

DIGGING DEEPER

➤ Make a list of all the drugs you know, including medicines and alcohol. Try to place them in an ordered list, from least harmful to most harmful. Discuss your lists together as a group.

➤ Looking at your list, can you decide on where the line is that you think people shouldn't cross? Which drugs are acceptable and which aren't? Why? What other factors are important?

➤ What do you think would happen if drugs such as cannabis were legalized and easily available?

TAKING IT TO THE WORD

➤ **Read** James 2:14–19.

➤ How could the principle of these verses have been applied to Ben? How do they apply to you?

➤ What happens when we talk about or say we believe in something, but our actions don't reflect it? What do others think? What does God think?

➤ Do you practise what you preach? Give examples of ways in which you do, and ways in which you don't.

➤ Pray for each other, that God will equip you to walk the walk, instead of just talking the talk.

A23

THEME: **Advertising**

BIBLE: **1 Thessalonians 1**

Advertising the church

'If a chocolate bar advert can promise "a taste of paradise", isn't it time for the church to do the same and more?' That was the question posed by *Christianity* magazine in an article called 'Advertising the Church'. They recruited the help of two major advertising agencies, commissioning them to design an imaginary poster campaign to encourage people to go to church.

The first company, Link ICA, designed three posters around the slogan 'Get a life – go to church'. Each featured the cross as part of medically themed artwork, suggesting that the church can 'save' your life. Another agency, Khameleon, came up with the campaign 'Church: you don't know what you're missing', encouraging people to 'enjoy some really good stand up for free' (a preacher) and 'really feel a part of the community'.

It's not an entirely new idea, of course. Bradford's Abundant Life Church already buys large advertising hoardings at the Bradford Bulls rugby stadium, in order to increase their community visibility. But, rather obviously, it's not cheap...

OPENING UP

➤ Do you think the church should advertise? Why or why not?

➤ What do you think of the advertising slogans that Link ICA and Khameleon came up with? Would they persuade your friends to come to church? Why or why not?

➤ What elements of the church do you think are worth shouting about?

DIGGING DEEPER

➤ How do you feel about advertising? Are adverts an irritation, or often better than the programmes, articles, etc. that they're placed around?

➤ Which adverts stick in your mind? Which ones do you like/dislike, and why?

➤ How many adverts – of all kinds – do you think you are exposed to in a day? Why not try to count them tomorrow?

TAKING IT TO THE WORD

➤ **Read** 1 Thessalonians 1:2–10.

➤ What kind of advertising is described here?

➤ Does this passage make you think the church should advertise? If so, how; if not, why?

➤ Design your own advertising campaign for your local church. You could even ask the minister if it can be used for real!

A24
THEME: **Rules**
BIBLE: **Exodus 20**

Shotgun rules

It's an age-old problem. You and your companions are getting a lift somewhere, and none of you wants to sit in the back. But there's only one space up front – how on earth do you decide who gets it?

'Calling shotgun' is a teenage tradition, dating back to the 1950s, which was set up to try to deal with this issue. Young people who didn't want to ride in the back would call out to claim their right to 'ride shotgun' in the passenger seat (the term was taken from covered wagons and the Wild West). After a while, though, as the practice became more and more popular, some confusion began to emerge. At what point were you allowed to 'call shotgun'? What if two of you called it simultaneously?

To answer these questions, the Shotgun Rules were established. They've been refined over the years, and are now listed at www.shotgunrules.com. They include 'the barefoot rule' (you can't call shotgun until you have your shoes on), 'the re-entry rule' (shotgun expires if you go back into the house before leaving), and 'the line-of-sight rule' (you must be able to see the car when calling). Widely respected among teenage motor passengers everywhere, these simple laws have once again restored order to the world of shotgun.

OPENING UP

➤ Have you ever used the shotgun rules? Do they work? Why or why not?

➤ These rules were created to preserve fun, rather than limit it. Can you think of other rules or laws which do this?

DIGGING DEEPER

➤ What other areas of your life involve rules? What kind of rules do you follow in your home life, your relationships, your school or in sports?

➤ How would these things be different if you didn't have any rules for them?

➤ If you were the lawmaker in your country, what rules and laws would you change, and which would you introduce?

TAKING IT TO THE WORD

➤ **Read** Exodus 20:1–21.

➤ Which of these rules might limit your enjoyment of life, and which might improve it? Explain your answers.

➤ Why do you think God gave these rules to his people after leading them out of slavery in Egypt?

➤ How well do you do at obeying this list? What might you score out of ten?

➤ Pick one of the commandments which you know you often break – pray together, asking God to help you to keep it in future.

A25

THEME: **Graffiti**

BIBLE: **Hebrews 11**

Making your mark

It developed into a whole new art form, spawned various fashion crazes and prevented many people from painting their houses white. More than twenty years after it first arrived in the UK, graffiti tagging is alive and well, and in some areas more prevalent than ever. The practice, where 'taggers' develop their own unique spray-paint signature and attempt to spread it as widely as possible, has become so common that the Government have been called into action – putting a bounty on the heads of the most prolific graffiti artists.

The Home Office's new 'Name That Tag' campaign offers a reward of £500 to anyone who can identify one of twelve repeat offenders from their 'tag' signatures. These are displayed on a series of posters in tube and train stations across Manchester, Liverpool and London, which invite members of the public to call in and give information on the offenders behind the tags. To qualify for inclusion in the 'dirty dozen', taggers will have vandalized literally hundreds of vehicles and buildings, contributing to a huge removal cost for the taxpayer. Graffiti removal costs London Underground alone £13 million a year.

OPENING UP

➤ What is your experience of graffiti? Where have you seen it? What do you feel about it?

➤ Why do you think graffiti artists feel the need to leave their mark?

➤ In what other, less destructive ways could they do this?

DIGGING DEEPER

➤ How do you want people to remember you? What do you hope to achieve in your life that will be remembered? Explain your answers.

➤ Graffiti is about creative expression – which some would say is mis-directed. How do you channel and express your creativity?

➤ How could you channel/express it better or differently?

TAKING IT TO THE WORD

➤ **Read** Hebrews 11:32–40. (Being listed in the Bible doesn't quite count as ancient graffiti, but these people have certainly made and left their mark.)

➤ Why are these people remembered?

➤ What is the equivalent today of 'shutting the mouths of lions' or 'facing jeers and flogging'?

➤ How can we use these examples in learning to make our own, positive mark on the world?

➤ If you are involved in illegal graffiti, confide in someone you can trust, and ask them to pray for you, to help you give it up.

Section B
Teen Issues

Introduction

Young people unavoidably face a complex moral maze. Conflicting voices from friends, family, the media and other sources send their heads spinning on a range of issues – from sexuality to ethics, from friendship rules to behaviour. As youth workers, we can help them to navigate a path through opinion, advice and belief, hopefully preventing them from getting too burnt along the way.

Story and discussion provide great, safe forums to explore the vital pressures and issues that young people face. Without having to go through an experience, young people are able to empathize with those who have, and hopefully learn and shape their own thinking in the process. With this in mind, the next twenty-five discussion starters all feature teenage characters. Some of these stories are fictional, others are based on true stories. All aim to open up a contemporary issue for debate and discussion.

In this section especially, the 'Digging deeper' questions are designed to help you move away from the story, and back into the reality of young people's own lives. The questions explore how the theme affects the young people, their friends and their community, and so they rarely refer to the story which they follow. The two threads are then pulled together again in the 'Taking it to the Word' questions.

Some of the stories, such as those which focus on issues like Sabbath or accepting homosexuality, are aimed specifically at Christian groups.

There are certain issues, like these, which are much more relevant to young people who have an experience and understanding of church and Christian culture, and so these discussion starters are likely to be less useful in unchurched contexts.

In this area particularly, it's possible that some significantly sensitive areas will be covered, and this could lead to unexpected pastoral needs arising within members of the group. For example, several of the discussions touch on the subject of divorce – this may be something that is particularly impacting on the lives of some of the young people in your group at this time. That's not to say that it won't be appropriate or helpful to discuss these issues with them, and allow them to have their say and express their hurt or other feelings. However, you should try wherever possible to evaluate each discussion against your group, attempt to calculate in advance the kind of unexpected impacts it might have, and prepare in advance for what might result. Whether that means having people on standby to counsel or pray, or changing the size or demographic profile of your group, is entirely up to you to decide.

Don't let that gentle warning put you off, however. These discussion starters provide a great opportunity for you to get to grips with the lives of your young people, and the unique local youth culture in which they reside. Even more importantly, they're designed to help young people to think through their beliefs, their morality and their ideas about the world. Get ready for some unexpected results...

B1

THEME: **Music piracy**

BIBLE: **Luke 16**

Download and burn

It was a great day in Geoff's life. He'd worked twelve consecutive Saturdays at the local coffee shop, and not spent a penny of his earnings. Now, the day had arrived when he could plough it all into his dream machine – a shiny new iPod, onto which he could download as much new music as he liked.

That night, he logged onto an official music website, and began downloading. But at 79p a track, it wasn't long before Geoff's very limited cash had run out. It was then that he stumbled upon a free file-sharing website. Here he could download almost every album ever recorded – and all for free! There was just one drawback, though: the website was illegal, and to download from it would amount to theft.

Geoff's iPod is now almost completely full of illegally downloaded tracks. But while digital music doesn't weigh anything, for some reason it feels rather heavy in his pocket.

OPENING UP

➤ Geoff saved up a lot of money for the iPod – so is what he did wrong? Why or why not?

➤ Why does Geoff feel guilty? What do you think he should do now?

➤ Decide as a group what your position is on illegal download-ing/copying music.

DIGGING DEEPER

➤ Why is theft generally seen as wrong? What are the conse-quences?

➤ But what about digital theft like this, or CD/tape copying – is that really hurting anyone? What might the consequences of that be? For someone like Geoff? For the music companies?

➤ Do you own, or want to buy a digital music player? Where will you get your music from?

TAKING IT TO THE WORD

➤ **Read** Luke 16:10–12.

➤ Discuss this passage. How does it shed light on what Jesus might say on this issue? What might be the consequences of (a) illegally downloading music or (b) refusing to do so?

➤ Get into pairs with someone you can talk to. Be honest – have you downloaded music illegally? Or copied your friend's albums onto tape? What's the group's agreed position on this issue? Pray together that you'll stick to this.

B2
THEME: **Laziness**
BIBLE: **Proverbs 6**

Lazy bones

Jake had a reputation of which he was very proud. Of all his friends, there was no one who could rival his ability to sleep in on a Saturday or Sunday morning. Any time before midday was unthinkable to him; getting up at 3 p.m. was quite normal. Sometimes, when it was the school holidays, he would even stay in bed for an entire day, never having to leave its warm comfort behind, thanks to his doormat mother, his TV remote and his extra-long PlayStation control-wire. If it hadn't been for the necessary toilet breaks, Jake may have spent whole weeks festering in his own dead skin cells.

Jake's friends used to find this amusing, but after a time, it became increasingly frustrating to them. His reluctance to emerge at a reasonable hour meant they had to play football later, and they never got to go to a morning church service because he always insisted that they went in the evening. Then, one day, they decided to change the time of their football game to 11 a.m., and lazy Jake missed out. A few weeks later, another member of the group, Clare, was singing in the morning church service, and everyone went along to support her. Except Jake. So now when they did most things together, Jake wasn't there, and before long, they'd begun to forget about him altogether. Jake is still proud of his laziness, but now, when he does get out of bed, his friends are nowhere to be seen.

OPENING UP

➤ Are you like Jake? Do you know people like him? Why do people spend so long in bed?

➤ What could Jake have been doing more usefully with his time?

➤ Why do you think young people get tired?

➤ If not taken to extremes like this, do you think it's OK to lounge around in bed? Why or why not?

DIGGING DEEPER

➤ Do you think you make good use of your time? How could you be better in this area?

➤ Think of some things you'd really like to achieve, do or see, but have never got round to.

➤ Make a hit-list of targets for yourself for the next year, for things you could achieve in that time. This might include going to see a favourite band or sporting team, saving up for something or creating something like a piece of art or a local project. It might just be investing time in a relationship, or reading a book that has been sat on your shelf! Put the list somewhere prominent, and try to come back to it from time to time to check how you're doing.

TAKING IT TO THE WORD

➤ **Read** Proverbs 6:6–11.

> ➤ Do these words shock you? Why or why not?

> ➤ Does it mean that we shouldn't rest?

> ➤ What's the lesson to be learned from ants?

> ➤ Why do you think the writer (Solomon) makes so much of this?

> ➤ Are you cramming too much in? If you need to, help one another to restructure your time, so that you properly balance work and rest. (Remember, God's ideal was always that we had a Sabbath rest-day every week.)

B3

THEME: Unrequited love

BIBLE: John 3

Not so Super for Mario

Mario was in love for the first time. He'd met Annika when they were both on holiday in America, and when he got back home to Italy, he couldn't stop thinking about her. Although he was only 15, Mario felt that this girl was special, and that they were meant to be together. That's why, just for a chance to see her again, he hitch-hiked 1,250 miles from Milan to Stockholm in Sweden.

Well, almost. In fact, he was picked up by police at a service station only 100 miles short of his final destination. Of course, Mario had travelled too far now to be sent back home, so he told officers that he was meeting his girlfriend and gave them her telephone number. One quick phone call later, Annika's father was on his way to collect Mario.

Alas, the story was not to have a romantic ending. Annika's father didn't take Mario home, but instead to the airport – on his daughter's instructions. Apparently she'd already decided that her time with the love-struck Italian had been no more than a swiftly forgotten holiday romance, and had asked her father to get rid of him.

OPENING UP

➤ How strongly do you think Mario must have felt about Annika to do this?

➤ How could Mario have got it so wrong?

➤ Mario lacked self-awareness: he couldn't see reality through his infatuation. Have you ever been involved in that sort of situation?

DIGGING DEEPER

➤ Do you think it's better to tell someone how you feel – and risk finding out the harsh reality – or to live on in romantic hope?

➤ What might have been a better way for Mario to approach this situation?

➤ How could Mario and Annika have treated each other better?

➤ How easy do you find it to speak truthfully, but in a positive and loving way (see Ephesians 4:15)?

TAKING IT TO THE WORD

➤ **Read** John 3:16 – notice particularly the words, 'God so loved the world...'

➤ How strongly do you think God must have felt about us to do this? Why do you think the creator of the universe would do something so big for tiny people like us?

➤ Jesus died for everybody, yet most people reject his love. How do you think that makes him feel?

➤ What might your response to this verse be?

B4

THEME: **The Sabbath**

BIBLE: **Exodus 20**

Workaholic

Clare loves fashion. She's not obsessed with labels, but she does enjoy nothing more than picking out colours and designs so that she can set her own trends. Trouble is, Clare comes from a poor family – the sort of loving but penniless home where a Christmas stocking contains an apple and an orange. So, although she's only 16, she has to work on Saturdays if she wants to buy just a few new items a month.

She's found out that fashion is depressingly expensive, though, and so when the manager at the store where she works – a clothes store, of course – offers her some Sunday hours too, she takes them. Even though she's a Christian, she's decided that she needs the money, if only so that she can keep up with her fashion-conscious friends. Now she works for almost all of the weekend.

Clare won't compromise on church – she finishes work on Sunday at 5 p.m. and is always showered, changed and ready in time for the evening service and the youth group time which follows it – but she is getting more and more tired. The latest designs are making her look pretty good... but the bags under her eyes certainly aren't.

OPENING UP

➤ Clare has a difficult problem – she's poor in an age of materialism. What would you do in her (trendy) shoes?

➤ List the pros and cons of what Clare is doing. Which list is longer?

➤ How might Clare re-order her life to get more rest?

DIGGING DEEPER

➤ Do you rest enough? What do you do in order to properly rest?

➤ How important is resting to you? Do you have a whole day in your week when you don't do any work of any kind? Why or why not?

➤ What forms of rest and relaxation do you think are most helpful to your mind, body and spirit, and which are perhaps less helpful? Where do playing sport, going to church, watching TV and lying in bed fit on that scale?

TAKING IT TO THE WORD

➤ **Read** Exodus 20:8–11.

➤ This is the classic reference used to argue against Sunday trading. What does it mean to you today?

➤ The Sabbath isn't actually Sunday, but some time between Friday and Saturday. Does that make it OK to work on Sundays? Why or why not?

➤ Why do you think God wants us to take a rest day?

➤ Where do you stand on Sunday trading? What about working on Sunday?

B5

THEME: Pornography

BIBLE: 1 Thessalonians 5

Dirty little secret

For his 16th birthday, Mike's parents had bought him the most incredible present: a state-of-the-art PC with a top graphics card, a lightning-speed processor and an in-built DVD player. At the same time, they decided to connect their home to Broadband Internet, so that Mike would be able to use his new computer to download notes and information to help him revise for his GCSEs. Mike was overjoyed – although his excitement was more connected to the possibilities of intercontinental *Doom* death matches than the homework help.

One day, however, when Mike really was searching for mock maths tests, he decided to put a few, well, different search terms into Google. What he got back was a stream of highly explicit photographs, and even movie footage of people having sex.

A month later, Mike was completely addicted. He'd got into the pattern of coming home, locking his room and looking at pornography every single night. Sometimes, he'd look more than once. His desire had become insatiable.

As a Christian, Mike feels dirty and sinful, but can't

stop himself from looking again and again. He's prayed about it, but his will just doesn't seem to be strong enough. He feels like he's locked into a cycle of sin, and in his better moments, he wishes that the computer had never arrived.

OPENING UP

➤ What advice would you give to Mike if he confided in you about this situation?

➤ What strategies could he use to protect himself against the 'cycle of sin'?

➤ Why do you think it hasn't saved him?

➤ What might the consequences be if this behaviour continues for a long time?

➤ Is what Mike is doing definitely wrong? Is it, as some doctors say, perfectly healthy? Why or why not?

DIGGING DEEPER

➤ Do you think the making and watching of pornography hurts anyone? Why or why not – and if so, who does it hurt?

➤ Why do you think people – 'actors', 'actresses' and 'models' – get involved in making porn? How do you think they feel about their involvement, and how might they feel about it later on in life?

➤ What do you think will happen to the role of pornography in our culture? Will it become bigger or smaller? Will the boundaries expand or contract?

TAKING IT TO THE WORD

➤ **Read** 1 Thessalonians 4:3–8.

> ➤ What might God feel about Mike's situation? How realistic do you think these verses are today?

> ➤ How do you think God feels about Mike? (Romans 3:22–24 may help here.)

> ➤ If this is an issue for you, consider becoming accountable by telling someone you can trust. Or if you are the person who is confided in, make sure you're a real friend and avoid laughing at or judging the other person.

B6

THEME: **Parents**

BIBLE: **Colossians 3/Ephesians 6**

Honour this father and mother?

Bethany has lived her whole life on a run-down housing estate which lies almost forgotten on the edge of a major city. It's a place where people drink a lot, get into fights and pin their hopes on horses called Lucky Ned and Lightning Jack (who never seem to live up to their names), mainly because the rest of their lives are so hard. Two of the biggest fighters, drinkers and gamblers are Bethany's mum and dad, but that never seemed strange to Bethany because it's what she grew up with.

Then, after a youth event on the estate, Bethany became a Christian, and suddenly her views started to change. The closer she seemed to get to God, and to her new friends from the 'nice part of town', the more alien her fighting, drinking, gambling parents began to look. When her mum staggered home drunk now, Bethany could no longer bear to help her to her bed. And when her dad decided to get satellite TV installed, even though he'd just lost his job, the last shred of respect she had for him simply evaporated.

In her heart, Bethany knows that the Bible tells her

to 'honour thy father and mother' – but in her head, she can't believe that God wants her to honour *these* parents.

OPENING UP

➤ Do you sympathize with Bethany, or feel she's being unfair?

➤ Why do you think her parents act the way they do? What might a truly Christian response be to these causes?

➤ What does it mean to 'honour' your parents? Do you think we should honour our parents more when they 'deserve it' because of the way they behave?

GOING DEEPER

➤ How much of an impact do you think parents have on the problems of teenagers?

➤ How do you think the average young person regards their parents? Why is this?

➤ What kind of parent do you think you would be? Are there any definite ideas that you have about how to be a good parent?

TAKING IT TO THE WORD

➤ **Read** Colossians 3:20–21 and Ephesians 6:1–4.

➤ How do you feel about the command to children here?

➤ In both cases, the verses talk about a parent's responsibility too – so what if they're not doing their bit?

➤ What advice would you give to Bethany in the light of these verses?

B7

THEME: # Talents and abilities
BIBLE: # Luke 19

Thicky's hidden talent

Darren Bastin never put much effort in at school. His nickname there was 'Thicky', and he decided to live down to it. Darren always knew what he wanted to do when he left – follow in his father's footsteps and become a lorry driver with Nuttall's Transport in Rochdale. With that end in mind, he left high school with no GCSEs, and didn't even bother to check the results of the three leaver's exams he had taken. A few years later, however, Darren realized that he'd made the wrong decision. Relentless weeks of long-distance driving began to bore him senseless, to the point where he was admitted to hospital with severe depression.

In hospital, Darren's brain more than recuperated. In fact, it began to flourish, as he at last decided to put it to work. First, for fun, he attempted a test created by the egg-heads' organization Mensa, and to his shock, he passed. Then, a few weeks later, he sat an official Mensa test and passed that too – placing his intellect in the top 2 per cent of the British population.

Darren kept his place among the geniuses quiet for nearly five years, before deciding to go to college. There he passed his GCSEs with flying colours, and decided to take the equivalent of three A-Levels. Suddenly, the lorry driver once known as 'Thicky' found himself at an entrance interview at a prestigious university. The egg-heads loved him. In September 2005, he started a history degree at Hughes Hall, part of the University of Cambridge.

OPENING UP

➤ What effect do you think Darren's nickname had on him? What does this tell us about the way we respond to the expectations of others?

➤ What do you think his peers think about his success? How do you think he feels? Would he regret not trying harder at school?

➤ Do you have a hidden talent that you're not developing? Share it with the person next to you, and discuss why you keep it hidden.

DIGGING DEEPER

➤ On your own, take a moment to list the skills and abilities that you feel you have. Then, encourage at least three other people about the talents that you feel they have. Try to encourage as many people as you can, and don't pick the most obvious people or abilities. Think hard – your words could have a real impact!

➤ What obstacles are there to recognizing your talents? And what can happen when you are too aware of those talents?

➤ Would you say that you make full use of the abilities that you have been given? Why or why not?

TAKING IT TO THE WORD

➤ **Read** Luke 19:12–26.

➤ Do you think the master was fair or unfair to his servants when he returned? Why?

➤ What does this parable tell us about God's attitude to the things he has given us? How does it apply to money, possessions and talents?

➤ Discuss this story as a metaphor for the way we use our God-given abilities. If appropriate, pray and commit together that you'll use yours in the right way.

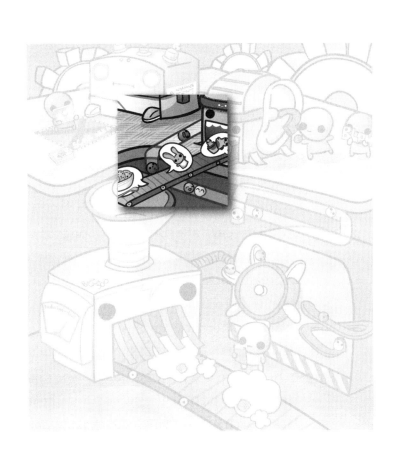

B8

THEME: **Integrity**

BIBLE: **Luke 16**

The cash stash

Jack Benson had been saving hard for months. Approaching his 17th birthday, he knew that his mum couldn't afford to pay for driving lessons – let alone a car. So for the past year, he'd been working hard in a crushingly dull Saturday job – the only way he could make sure he'd be on the road in time for the summer.

One Saturday, after another boring day at work, Jack was getting the train home when he noticed a plastic bag under his seat. Pulling it out, he was shocked to discover that it was stuffed full of £50 notes! Noticing that there was no one nearby, Jack gazed into the bag and imagined what he could do with all that cash. His dream of a rusty old banger was rapidly being replaced by the picture of a second-hand sports car!

Jack took the bag home, and thought some more. He knew that if he kept this money, he could give up his boring Saturday job and book the driving lessons now. He also knew that if he was careful, he'd probably never even get caught. It didn't seem right to him, though, and he handed the bag in to the police. Now he'll only be able to buy an old banger, but at least he won't feel guilty about it.

OPENING UP

➤ What do you think of Jack's decision? What would you have done in his shoes? Be as honest as you can!

➤ Why do you think Jack made that choice? What factors might have influenced him?

➤ Name someone whose integrity you respect. Why that person?

DIGGING DEEPER

➤ How much would it cost to get you to do the following: tell a lie; eat a sheep's brain; punch a stranger in the face; sing at the top of your voice in a packed train carriage?

➤ What are the values and beliefs that you would try never to give up on or deny? Who are the people you would try to stand up for at any cost?

➤ Would you be prepared to lay down your life for any of the people above? Explain your answer.

TAKING IT TO THE WORD

➤ **Read** Luke 16:10–15.

➤ What do you think this passage suggests Jack should have done with the money?

➤ This passage isn't just about money. What do you think are the wider implications of Jesus' words?

➤ Pray together, asking God to help you to be people of integrity.

B9

THEME: ## Sexual guilt

BIBLE: ## Matthew 19

Under pressure

Mark and Karen had been going out for nearly a year. The rest of their youth group had begun to refer to them as 'Mr and Mrs', and their relationship had become a cornerstone of their friendship group. After three months, they'd said 'I love you' to each other for the first time, and after six months, they'd even gone on holiday together, with Karen's family. They were really serious about each other, and despite the jokes, had already begun to talk about marriage, even though they were both only 16.

Both Mark and Karen had been Christians since they were young, and both publicly stated that they felt sex was for marriage only. Privately though, Mark was finding it more and more difficult to hold to that belief. As slowly their relationship became more and more passionate, Mark began to suggest to Karen that, since they were going to get married one day anyway, they should start to have sex.

At first she was shocked, and extremely against the idea. However, after Mark applied more and more pressure, she eventually gave in. When Mark's parents went away for the weekend, they seized the opportunity to sleep together.

The next day, Karen realized that she'd made a terrible mistake. She'd lost her virginity, and now she couldn't bring it back. She was soon in floods of tears. Seeing her distress, Mark also began to regret what they had done. And although they tried hard to rescue it, and promised not to sleep together again, the relationship fell apart soon afterwards.

OPENING UP

➤ What do you think about Karen's reaction? Do you think it was over the top? Why or why not?

➤ What steps could or should they have taken to stop things from going so far?

➤ Do you think Mark and Karen were ready for a sexual relationship at 16? If yes, what if one or both of them were 15 – would that change your view?

DIGGING DEEPER

➤ Why do you think some people wait to have sex until they are married? Why do others do it much earlier? What do you think is the right age or time?

➤ What do you think might be the consequences of having sex with lots of different people through the course of your life? Are there any major advantages or disadvantages?

➤ How would you feel if the person you had married had slept with twenty people before you? What if they'd never slept with anyone?

TAKING IT TO THE WORD

➤ **Read** Matthew 19:4–6.

> ➤ These verses come in the context of Jesus' teaching on adultery – why are they relevant to this story?
>
> ➤ If through sex, two people become one, what are the implications for people who have lots of sexual partners?
>
> ➤ Why do you think God intends us to only have one sexual partner?

B10

THEME: Peer pressure/drugs

BIBLE: 1 Peter 4

Just a few puffs...

Claire's parents had left her home alone for the first time, aged 15. While they made her promise not to host any wild parties in their absence, they did agree that she could invite a few of her girlfriends round for a sleepover. Happy with this compromise, Claire invited a group of her friends, bought a freezer-ful of pizza and ice-cream, and rented a couple of the latest DVDs for the slumber party.

Eight of her friends arrived, sleeping-bags in hand, along with a couple of other girls who were friends-of-friends. One of them, Imogen, quickly voiced her opinion that Claire's get together was 'a bit lame', and suggested they should spice things up a little. Unpacking her rucksack, she produced two large bottles of Jack Daniels and a bag of marijuana.

Imogen rolled several joints, and began passing them around the wide-eyed group of girls. Under pressure from her friends, Claire smoked some. At first, it had little effect, but after a couple of puffs, things changed. Her head began to spin, and combined with the effects of the alcohol, the drugs soon caused her to be physically sick in the middle of the room.

The mood of the party was ruined, and Claire was distraught. Imogen laughed at her for being a 'light-weight', and the rest of her friends teased her for giving in too easily to peer pressure. When her parents arrived home a few days later, they didn't find any trace of drink, drugs or Claire's regurgitated pizza. Still, their daughter was overcome with feelings of guilt, and desperately wished she'd been stronger.

OPENING UP

➤ What are your views on drug use? What's OK to take, and what's not? Does it matter how old you are?

➤ Who do you think you are most like in the story – Claire, Imogen, or one of the other friends? Explain your answer.

➤ Do you think Claire was too hard on herself? Why or why not?

➤ What could Claire have said or done to relieve the pressure that her friends put on her?

DIGGING DEEPER

➤ How big an influence is peer pressure in your life? Is it a major factor in your school, college or friendship group?

➤ What does peer pressure look and feel like?

➤ Do you ever put pressure on others? If so, how and why?

TAKING IT TO THE WORD

➤ **Read** 1 Peter 4:1–7.

➤ What do these verses say about peer pressure? Look particularly at verse 4.

➤ How realistic do you think these verses are? Why?

➤ Why do Christians have to fight against peer pressure? What help can they get to do this?

B11

THEME: Attitudes to homosexuality

BIBLE: Galatians 6

Forced into the margin

Carl had been a member of the St George's youth group since he was 11 years old. By age 17, he had become one of the core members of the group – one of the young people who the younger teens looked up to, and who the youth workers were grooming for future leadership. All that changed, however, when Carl decided to be honest about something.

Carl met with two other guys from the group each week to pray and talk about their lives. When it was Carl's turn to share, he admitted that he had something very important and very confidential to say. He'd been feeling something for a long time, and he finally had to tell someone: he was gay.

Carl's friends tried to hide their shock, fear and even disgust. They managed to stutter through a few words of prayer for him, and then quickly said their goodbyes. Carl was hurt by their response, even though he'd expected it.

Within minutes, one of Carl's prayer partners was on the phone to the youth worker, who urged him to keep this information private. The gossip was simply too exciting, however, and within hours he'd told several friends, from whom the news spread like wildfire.

The next night at youth group, Carl was getting strange looks from every angle. In one evening, he had been ripped from the centre of the group and shunted into the margins. His good friends couldn't even look at him. It was the last time he ever went to the youth group, or the church.

OPENING UP

➤ How does this story make you feel?

➤ Who do you feel is to blame for Carl leaving the group? Why?

➤ How do you think the different characters in this story could have handled things better?

DIGGING DEEPER

➤ How do you feel about: homosexual people; homophobic people? Try to explain the reasons for those feelings.

➤ How do you think you would react if a really close friend told you (and perhaps only you) that they were gay? What would or wouldn't change in your relationship?

➤ How do you think our culture feels about gay people? Do you think that feeling has changed/is changing?

TAKING IT TO THE WORD

➤ **Read** Galatians 6:1–6.

> ➤ What does this passage suggest about a Christian approach to homosexual people?

> ➤ What does it mean to carry each other's burdens in a situation like this?

> ➤ How does the church famously make the mistake warned about in verse 3, with particular regard to this issue?

> ➤ Verse 4 is a helpful reminder that 'all have sinned and fall short of the glory of God'. Pray together that you'll never become judgmental, but seek to honestly build each other up instead.

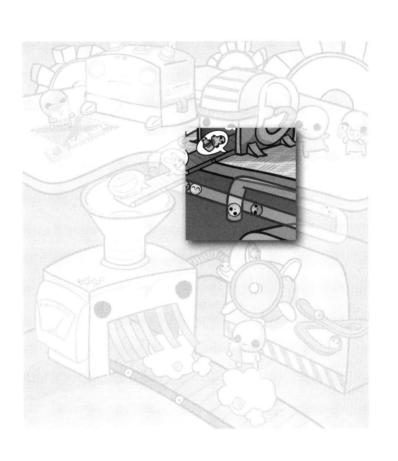

B12
THEME: **Stealing**
BIBLE: **Matthew 6**

The free CD

It was the end of the month, and Lisa didn't have a penny to her name. It was a whole week before her parents would hand over her generous pocket money again, and no amount of begging convinced them that they should give her an advance. It meant that she couldn't join her friends at the cinema on Saturday night; it meant that she'd have to wait to buy the new top she wanted. It was very frustrating.

With five days to go until parent-pay-day, Lisa was in her local newsagent, and noticed the latest copy of *Music Weekly*. It had the words 'Free CD' emblazoned across the cover, and underneath, an exclusive acoustic album recorded by her favourite band in the whole world. Although the CD was 'free', the magazine cost five pounds. And even worse than that – by the time she got her pocket money, this issue would no longer be available.

Lisa thought for a moment. The magazine might be out of her price range, but according to the label, the CD was technically 'free'. Seeing that the cashier was busy, she gently detached the album from the magazine cover, and slipped it into her coat. She left the shop undetected, with a big smirk on her face. She'd never shoplifted before, but then this wasn't really stealing – was it?

OPENING UP

➤ Since the CD was free, do you think this was really stealing? Why?

➤ Can you identify with Lisa's frustration at having no money?

➤ What might you have done in her shoes?

➤ Do you think Lisa might have now considered stealing other things? Why or why not?

➤ Do you think shoplifting is as serious as other crimes? Explain your answer.

DIGGING DEEPER

➤ What's your view of debt? Are you relaxed about it, or scared? Why?

➤ Do you find it difficult to save money? Why or why not?

➤ Do you find that there are lots of financial pressures on you? Where do these come from?

➤ How often do you seem to need to spend money? What influences this?

TAKING IT TO THE WORD

➤ **Read** Matthew 6:19–21.

➤ What do these verses say to us about stealing?

➤ What does verse 21 suggest is really going on when we steal?

➤ What else can we learn from these verses? How should they impact on the way that we live in a materialistic age?

B13

THEME: Acceptance

BIBLE: Acts 9

The new kid

Class 9JB had been together for three years, and had gained a reputation in their school as a 'nice class'. Teachers liked them; there were no trouble-makers; everyone got on with one another. And in that time, no one had left the class, and no one had joined it. They were a settled group who liked their school and each other.

Then, one day towards the end of their third year together, the teacher announced that a new boy was joining 9JB from a different school. Some of the class, including a Christian named Dez, got ready to welcome the newbie, but their faces fell when they laid eyes on him. With his ghostly pale skin and jet-black hair, it was immediately clear that he wasn't going to fit in with the group of trendies, townies and sk8ers who made up 9JB.

The welcome party disbanded, and the new boy, Zach, drifted to a lonely desk at the back of the room. He looked particularly depressed as the rest of the class stared at him as if he was from another planet.

The school day began, and for the entire morning, no one managed to say a single word to him.

In the dining-hall at lunchtime, Dez felt really bad. His conscience was telling him to go and make friends with Zach, but his feet wouldn't move. He could tell that he and Zach wouldn't have much in common, and he didn't want to risk his own position of popularity in the class. Seeing that Dez was looking at him, Zach offered a weak smile in his direction.

Dez turned away and headed off to the field to play football. He was sure someone else would go and make friends with the new kid eventually.

OPENING UP

➤ How does this story make you feel?

➤ What do you think Dez should have done differently? Why?

➤ If Dez is a Christian, is it his responsibility to make friends with Zach? Why or why not?

DIGGING DEEPER

➤ Have you ever been part of a big established group when someone who was different in some way tried to join? What happened?

➤ Have you ever been that outsider? How did you feel?

➤ What kinds of factors can make someone the outsider in a group? How do you think we should respond to these different types of people?

TAKING IT TO THE WORD

➤ **Read** Acts 9:23–28.

> ➤ Saul had overseen the persecution of many Christians – including the stoning of Stephen. How do you think the Christians felt when he was brought to them?

> ➤ Put yourself in Barnabas' shoes here – how would you have felt?

> ➤ What does this story tell us about how we should treat out-siders?

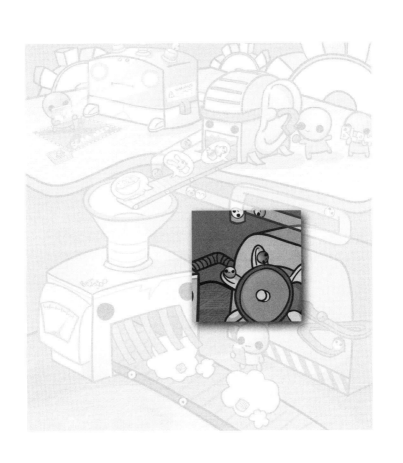

B14
THEME: **Cheating**

BIBLE: **Genesis 27**

◆ Testing times

Yasmin had been studying for her big maths test for almost a week. She'd worked unusually hard in class, and she'd even missed a trip to the cinema with her friends to stare at textbooks, but she was still having trouble with the subject.

The day of the test arrived and Yasmin started to work through the questions. Time passed, and as she glanced across she could see that the rest of her class were all filling up their exam sheets with mathematical scribbles. Yasmin couldn't concentrate. And when the first of her classmates left the room – test paper completed – Yasmin began to panic.

That's when she noticed that the girl to her left, Yi-Ling, had finished her test and was also leaving the room. Yi-Ling was one of the top maths students in the class, and now her exam sheet was just sitting there on her desk, almost certainly full of the correct answers. Yasmin knew it would be easy to reach over and copy those answers, but of course, that would be cheating.

Fortunately for her, the teacher didn't notice as Yasmin took her friend's paper and copied it, number for number. She left the exam room exhilarated, and when her excellent grade was duly awarded, her parents and teachers were impressed. Clearly, they said, all that hard study had paid off. Yasmin knew the truth, however, and not only did she now feel guilty that she had cheated on one test, she now knew that she would have to find a way to pass the next one... and the one after that.

OPENING UP

➤ Yasmin had studied hard for her test – does this slightly excuse her cheating?

➤ What might you have done in Yasmin's shoes?

➤ Do you think Yasmin would be tempted to stop studying and cheat on her next test?

DIGGING DEEPER

➤ Honesty time! Have you ever cheated at something – maybe not an exam – perhaps a game or some other piece of school work?

➤ How does it feel to cheat and get caught? (Or how do you imagine it feels?!)

➤ How do you think it feels to cheat and get away with it? What might the results be?

TAKING IT TO THE WORD

➤ **Read** Genesis 27:1–37.

➤ In this story, Jacob cheats Esau in order to receive his father's blessing. Where do you think the blame lies in this story?

➤ Do you feel sorry for Esau and/or Isaac? Why or why not?

➤ After this story, Jacob goes on to become a very important figure in history, and the Bible. Do you think this end justifies his means? Explain your answer.

➤ Read Ephesians 4:25. What does this verse tell us about the responsibility of Christians on this issue?

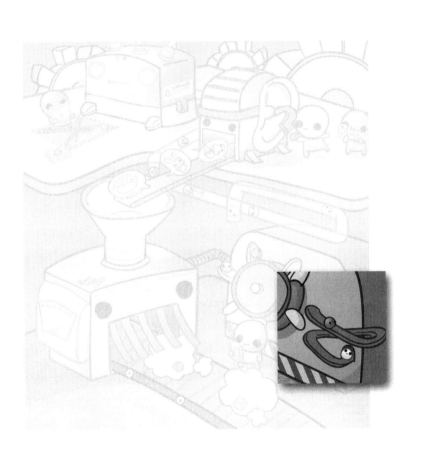

B15

THEME: **Television**

BIBLE: **Acts 17/Philippians 4**

Square eyes

The day Jake's dad got satellite TV installed was the day that Jake decided there must be a God. He had always enjoyed watching television, but now the viewing choices open to him were incredible. As long as it coincided with what his dad wanted to watch, Jake could spend three or four hours every night enjoying movies, live sports, and dozens of weekly drama and comedy shows. Even though it meant that he rarely went out with friends, he was in heaven.

Jake's mum came over one weekend, and realized how much television her son was watching. She told him that she was worried; it seemed like he was spending far too much time glued to the screen. Jake protested – he said he was learning from documentaries, and developing his imagination through watching movies and drama. His mum forced him to turn the television off for the afternoon, but as soon as her visit had ended, he switched it back on again.

To get back at his ex-wife, Jake's dad even went out and bought a separate satellite receiver box for his son's room. Now Jake never faces a battle for the remote control, and, with his television addiction completely fulfilled, rarely even leaves his bedroom.

OPENING UP

➤ How does this story make you feel? What kinds of issues does it raise?

➤ What would you say to Jake about his TV watching?

➤ Do you know anyone who has a TV addiction like Jake? What are the side-effects?

DIGGING DEEPER

➤ How much TV do you watch? Do you think that's too much, too little, or just about right?

➤ What are some of your favourite television programmes? Do you think these are a good or bad influence on you? Why?

➤ What kinds of influences do you think television programmes have on people – positive and negative?

TAKING IT TO THE WORD

➤ **Read** Acts 17:16–34 and Philippians 4:8–9.

➤ These two passages are among those most frequently used to justify or criticize Christians engaging with the media. Which do you find easiest to agree with – Paul's speech on Athenian culture, or his warning to keep our minds filled with things that are pure?

➤ Why do you think Paul communicated with the people in Athens in such a way? What do you think the reaction might have been?

➤ What might a modern equivalent of this conversation be for us?

➤ Does your media consumption match up with Philippians 4? If not, how do these verses challenge, irritate or confuse you?

➤ Pray together, that God will help you to work out what's right and wrong to watch on TV.

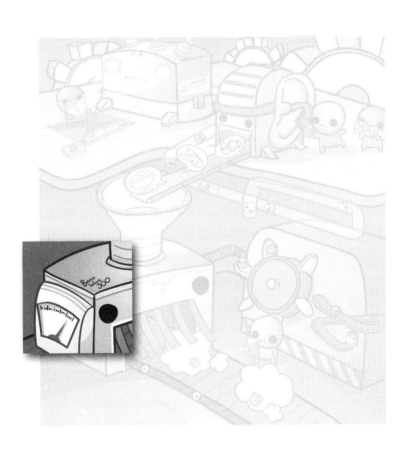

B16

THEME: ## Healthy relationships... good break-ups

BIBLE: ## Romans 13

Let's still be friends...

Kellie and Dennis had been going out for about six months when their relationship just seemed to run out of steam. Kellie started to like someone else, and Dennis was beginning to miss his freedom. There were no fireworks – no big battles – they just turned around to each other one day, and said, 'Let's stop.' It had been fun while it had lasted, but things had run their course.

The evening they split up, Dennis said the same thing to Kellie that he'd said (and never really meant) to every girl he'd ever been out with: 'Let's still be friends.' So he was quite taken aback, a week later, when Kellie called to ask him if he wanted to do something that weekend – just as friends.

Kellie wasn't trying to get the relationship back together – in fact she had started going out with the other guy she liked – but she'd taken Dennis at his word. They enjoyed a fun evening together, and promised each other they'd do it again some time.

Dennis' friends told him he was crazy to keep seeing Kellie, but he saw it differently. He was proud that for the first time in his life, breaking up with a girlfriend hadn't meant the loss of a friend.

OPENING UP

➤ How realistic do you think this story is? How do relationships usually end, and what can be some of the social consequences?

➤ How have you seen social groups impacted and changed by the ending of a relationship?

➤ How might groups such as those you've just mentioned be different if all break-ups were as amicable as this one?

➤ Do you think it's important to try hard to remain on good terms with people we used to go out with? Why or why not? What might some of the dangers be?

DIGGING DEEPER

➤ What's your philosophy on relationships? Is it OK to go out with several people at the same time... or should you only date someone you'd be prepared to marry? Explain as far as you feel comfortable.

➤ What can we learn from healthy dating relationships?

➤ What rules might help relationships to stay healthy?

TAKING IT TO THE WORD

➤ **Read** Romans 13:8–13.

➤ What helpful advice is contained in these verses that might ensure our relationships are healthy?

➤ What does verse 10 tell us about love? How does the love that you have given and received stand up to this acid test?

➤ How realistic is it to put aside your desires and focus on Jesus? What might help you to achieve this?

B17

THEME: # The Holy Spirit
BIBLE: # 1 Corinthians 14

Tongues twister

Jamie and Chris were Christians in the youth group of a small church. Both of them played in the church band, and so when a big worship event was announced in the nearby town, they decided to go along.

Both of them loved the upbeat worship (and wished they could play like that). They both enjoyed the speaker, a Bible teacher who also used to be a stand-up comedian. But when it came to the end of the service, their opinions were divided. The service leader announced that they would be having a 'prayer ministry time', where they would ask to be filled with the Holy Spirit.

Jamie wasn't so sure about this, and folded his arms in discomfort. Expecting Chris to do the same, however, he was shocked to see his friend with arms outstretched, shaking violently as the leader prayed. Quickly, two members of the 'prayer ministry team' stood either side of Chris, and laid hands on him in prayer. Jamie was feeling even more uncomfortable.

Then, even more startlingly, Chris opened his mouth, and started talking in a strange foreign language. He opened his eyes, laughed, and continued to 'speak in tongues'. Chris left the event walking on air, but his friend was furious. He felt like he'd spent the evening in a religious cult, and vowed never to go anywhere like that again.

OPENING UP

➤ Who would you have identified with in the story – Jamie or Chris? Explain your answer.

➤ What do you believe about the Holy Spirit? Do you think people who speak in tongues or fall over under the Spirit's power are faking it or are for real?

➤ What experiences do you have of the Holy Spirit – in your life or in the lives of people you know?

DIGGING DEEPER

➤ Do you believe in a supernatural side to the world? What does that look like to you?

➤ Do you think angels and demons exist? Do they have an influence in the world today?

➤ What is your view on the occult? Is it real? Is it dangerous?

➤ What do you think is the relationship between the occult and the angelic?

TAKING IT TO THE WORD

➤ **Read** 1 Corinthians 14.

➤ Do you think these verses apply to us today? Why or why not?

➤ What do we learn about the different spiritual gifts here?

➤ What rules and advice are there about the gift of tongues here? Why do you think this detailed advice is in here?

➤ What do we learn in the final part of the passage about order in Christian worship? Why do you think this is important?

B18
THEME: **Jealousy**
BIBLE: **1 Samuel 18**

The jealous guy

Jordan was one of the most popular kids at school, and not just because his dad was a millionaire. He was also good-looking, funny, generous and clever. People liked to be around him – and the fact that he always paid for the pizzas was just a bonus.

Joe found it difficult to like Jordan. As one of the *less* popular kids, he disliked Jordan for all the same reasons that most people loved to hang around with him. Joe wasn't very clever, he wasn't very good-looking, and he wasn't very funny. And coming from a poor family, he certainly wasn't able to afford a round of pizzas. So when he saw Jordan, all he was reminded of was what he didn't have.

One afternoon, Joe and Jordan both arrived late at their maths class. There were only two seats left, and so Jordan sat in the first. Joe gritted his teeth, cursed his bad luck, and sat down in the other.

Jordan was his usual friendly, helpful self, but all Joe could see was the assorted evidence of all the things Jordan had – from the 80GB iPod in his bag to the expensive watch on his wrist. From around the room, different friends would shout out to Jordan – and even the teacher liked him. Joe got angrier and angrier. He hated Jordan – it was so unfair that he had so much. Of course, he didn't say anything; he just sat there and smouldered.

At the end of the lesson, Jordan invited Joe to a party he was having at the weekend. Joe managed to fake a smile and thank him for the offer. Of course, he had no intention of going along whatsoever.

OPENING UP

➤ How does it make you feel when certain people seem to have everything going right for them? Is it unfair?

➤ What is your reaction to Joe? Do you feel sympathy for him? Or something else?

➤ What do you think is the bigger problem here – Jordan's wealth or Joe's jealousy? Why?

➤ What are the side-effects of Joe's jealousy in this story?

DIGGING DEEPER

➤ Do you ever feel jealous? What kind of things or people do you find you are jealous of?

➤ Is it ever right to be jealous? If so, in what circumstances?

➤ What do you think long-term jealousy does to a person? What might be a positive alternative?

TAKING IT TO THE WORD

➤ **Read** 1 Samuel 18:1–9.

➤ This story comes after David has defeated the giant Goliath. How do you think he would have viewed himself after this victory?

➤ Why do you think King Saul was jealous of David?

➤ Why was Saul concerned about losing his throne? Do you think he was right to be concerned?

➤ What are the feelings that you get about David and Saul from reading these verses? Where do you think this story is going?

➤ Who do you identify with in this story, and why? Who would you rather be?

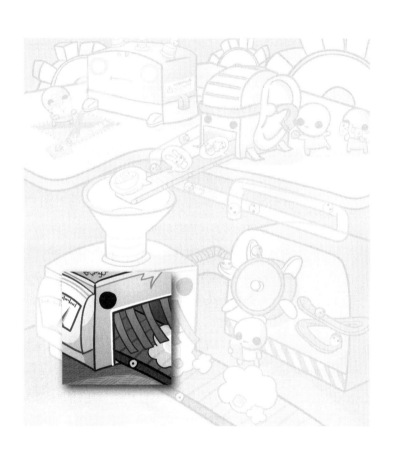

B19
THEME: **Dieting**
BIBLE: **Luke 15**

Dieting to be thin

Sara can't remember a time when she wasn't on a diet. She remembers being the slowest runner in gym class; she recalls her dad telling her not to eat too many biscuits; she can't forget the teasing she's always had to put up with about her weight. But she can't remember when she actually started dieting – only that she's been doing it non-stop ever since.

Sara doesn't have an eating disorder. She tries to eat healthily; often she fails, and ends up doing the opposite. She finds it hard to lose weight, and difficult to exercise. Of course, she's not that big – but growing up in a world where fashion magazine pages are full of tiny models, she's made to feel like she is.

Even though she's attractive, and always has boys interested in her, most days Sara feels like a fat pig. She writes her weight down in a diary every day, but it never changes very much. It seems like whatever diet she tries, nothing will take her down to the weight she dreams of.

Sara hopes that one day she'll achieve her perfect weight. Until then, she'll continue to plough all her money into slim-fast shakes, diet books and miracle pills, and dream about looking like a fashion model.

OPENING UP

➤ How does this story make you feel?

➤ Why do you think Sara is so obsessed with losing weight?

➤ Name some famous people who you think have healthy bodies, and others who you think look unhealthy. Explain why you think this about them.

➤ What do you think will happen to Sara in the future? Will she reach her target weight? How do you think she'll feel if she does?

➤ What kind of body would you like to have, and why?

DIGGING DEEPER

➤ Is healthy eating important to you? Why or why not?

➤ Do you feel you eat sensibly? What does that mean in practice?

➤ Do you think dieting is a good discipline? When can it be less positive?

➤ Why do you think so many people spend so much time on a diet?

TAKING IT TO THE WORD

➤ **Read** Luke 15:1–7.

➤ What does this story tell us about how God sees us?

➤ Is this illustration just about sin? If not, what else might be going on?

➤ How does this picture of God's love affect your own self-image?

B20

THEME: ## Violent video games

BIBLE: ## Colossians 3

In the game

For the first four years of his high-school life, everyone had always thought of Baz as a chilled-out and gentle guy. Even though he naturally had a muscular body, no one had ever seen him use it to create violence. Quick-witted and clever, he was the sort of person who let his mouth do the talking, rather than his fists.

As he grew older, bigger and even more muscular, however, Baz started to change. He became more physical with his friends, and then with his enemies. Suddenly, Baz was in the middle of every fight the school grounds had to offer.

After a few bouts of this behaviour, the school became concerned about Baz, and so the headmaster asked the boy's parents to come in for a chat. His dad had no idea what might have triggered this violent change in Baz's behaviour, but his mum saw it differently. She explained that since Christmas, a few months earlier, Baz had been spending a lot of time playing on his new games console. He only really bothered with one game, a super-violent beat-'em-up called *Battle Carnage*.

Baz's dad laughed off the suggestion that a video game might be responsible for his son's behaviour, and suggested it was probably all to do with hormones. His wife and the headmaster were not so sure.

OPENING UP

➤ Do you think there's a link between video-game violence and real-life violence? Why?

➤ Do you play video games? If so, how much do you think they can influence your behaviour?

➤ What might be a good way forward for Baz's parents in this story?

DIGGING DEEPER

➤ What kinds of video games are popular today? What kinds do you find most fun or exciting to play?

➤ Why do you think video games are so popular?

➤ Do you think people should follow age restrictions on games? If so, how closely should we stick to the guidance? If not, why not?

TAKING IT TO THE WORD

➤ **Read** Colossians 3:5–14.

➤ How much of the negative stuff mentioned in verses 5 and 8 do you find in the video games, movies, TV shows and music that you consume? What do you think the influence of these might be?

➤ How much of the positive stuff mentioned in verse 12 do you find in the same things? Are there certain areas of the media that offer this? Are you naturally attracted to them? Why or why not?

➤ Why do you think the writer, Paul, tells Christians to put the first set of things aside and focus on the second?

➤ Do you think the world would change if the media were full of the ideas in verse 12? If so, how?

B21

THEME:　Divorce

BIBLE:　James 3

A fight too far

Megan's parents had never managed to keep their many arguments private. Megan and her sisters had always had to sit around the dinner table, staring into space while their parents rowed about everything from her dad's affair to her mum's inability to cook vegetables. Almost every night, as far back as she could remember, there'd been something for them to shout at each other about.

Eventually, after her dad admitted to a second affair, Megan's mum could take no more and ordered him to move out. The next day, she called her daughters together, and explained that she'd asked their father for a divorce. Megan was shocked. Even though she'd always hoped that the arguments would stop one day, she had certainly never wanted this.

Since she heard that news from her mum, Megan has changed. Her performance at school has started to drop; she's become withdrawn in her social circle. She feels like no one understands what she's going through. Her mum is pressing ahead with the divorce, and just three months after throwing her husband out, has even started dating other men. Megan feels sick when they come round. Even though the house was always full of shouting, she wished things could be back the way they used to be.

OPENING UP

➤ How does this story make you feel?

➤ Have you or someone close to you gone through a situation like this? What was it like, and what were some of the effects? Share only what you feel comfortable talking about.

➤ What would be your advice to Megan at this point?

➤ Do you think Megan's mum should have waited before dating other men? Why?

DIGGING DEEPER

➤ Why do you think more and more people are getting divorced these days? What do you think is the impact of this on society?

➤ Do rising divorce rates change your attitudes to marriage? Why or why not?

➤ Do you think it's better to stay in an unhappy marriage, or get divorced? Why? What other options might there be?

TAKING IT TO THE WORD

➤ **Read** James 3:13–18.

➤ What does it mean to be a 'peacemaker' (verse 18)? What does this achieve?

➤ What advice might this passage provide to people who need to fix a broken relationship?

➤ Which definition of 'wisdom' more closely reflects you and what you are like? Which kind of wisdom would you prefer to exhibit? Why?

➤ Consider praying together, that God will help you to be wise, particularly in the area of relationships.

B22

THEME: Eating disorders

BIBLE: Psalm 139

Don't tell!

John and Evie had been best friends for as long as they could remember. They talked about everything together and had managed to get through all the awkwardness of a boy/girl friendship a long time ago.

Now, John was worried about Evie. For almost two years she had been worrying about her weight and constantly complaining about how she couldn't get a boyfriend because 'she was fat'. John knew Evie wasn't fat; in fact, he thought she was looking pretty skinny. At first he had thought her concerns were the same thing all girls felt, but now, as he watched her getting thinner and thinner, he was worried that maybe Evie was suffering from an eating disorder.

John knew that someone from school had talked to Evie's mum about her weight last year and that Evie's mum had got angry, saying that Evie had a high metabolism and just wanted to look her best. Now things were considerably worse; he knew Evie wasn't eating and had even seen diet pills in her bag.

When John saw Evie at lunch she refused to eat anything and showed him her diet pills. He tried to talk to her, but she insisted that being a boy, he wouldn't understand. She said that if he was really her friend, he had to accept that this was one thing he couldn't help her with.

OPENING UP

➤ Do you agree with Evie? Is this something he should leave to her female friends, and stay out of?

➤ Would John be breaking his loyalty to Evie if he told someone about her diet pills? If not, who should John talk to?

➤ Evie's mum doesn't seem to think there's a problem. Do you think adults always know best in this kind of situation? Explain your answer.

DIGGING DEEPER

➤ How good do you think your self-image is? Explain your answer.

➤ Where do people get their self-esteem from? Where do you get yours?

➤ What are some good places from which to draw your self-esteem? What might be some less good places?

➤ How can you help to improve one another's self-image?

TAKING IT TO THE WORD

➤ **Read** Psalm 139:1–16.

➤ What do these verses tell us about how God views us?

➤ Do you find this passage reassuring, or do you have a different reaction?

➤ What does the idea that you are 'fearfully and wonderfully made' (verse 14) do for your self-image? Explain your answer.

B23

THEME: **Fairness**

BIBLE: **Isaiah 33**

Unfair advantage

Jen had been playing on her school netball team for nearly two years. She wasn't the best player in her year, but she practised regularly and enjoyed being part of the team. Her older sister, Sophie, was on the sixth-form team and a bit of a star there. Sophie would help Jen when they practised in the garden together on weekends.

In her final year at school, Jen had an accident in one of the games and injured her ankle. She wasn't able to play for the rest of the year, or even practise during the summer holidays with her sister.

That autumn Jen moved up to the sixth form. Her injury had healed and she was ready to start playing netball again. Jen knew that the sixth-form team already had a strong line-up, even after her sister Sophie had graduated and left. Jen was willing to be patient and earn her position on the team through hard work and practice.

However, Jen was very surprised when the sixth-form netball coach announced she had been picked for the first game of the season, in the important goal-attack position. The coach had never seen Jen play before and knew she'd had an injury, which meant she hadn't been able to practise.

Embarrassed and guilty, Jen was sure the coach had given her such an important position on the team because she was Sophie's little sister. She looked around at her new team-mates, sure that they all knew why she'd been picked as well. Jen agreed to play – after all, it was what she wanted. The first game went well and Jen's team won. She was still a good player, but she was no star like her sister.

That night, at home, Jen talked to Sophie about the coach's decision. Jen wanted to step down from her place on the team and try to earn a position on merit. Sophie told her to just keep going: 'So what if you've got a bit of a free ride to the top! Now you're there, you might as well make the most of it.'

Jen felt trapped. If she stepped down, she'd lose the respect of her coach and maybe Sophie too. If she stayed, sooner or later her team-mates would figure out she wasn't the star player everyone expected her to be...

OPENING UP

➤ Is the coach right to give Jen an opportunity based on her sister's reputation?

➤ Have you ever seen someone benefit from an unfair situation? How did you feel about the results?

➤ How do you feel about Sophie's advice? Should Jen follow it? Why or why not?

DIGGING DEEPER

➤ Do you think it's more acceptable to profit from an unfair situation if you are not responsible for it? Explain your answer.

➤ List some examples of things in the world that aren't fair (for instance, unfair trade) – what should our reaction be to them?

➤ Is fairness the same as justice? Explain your answer.

TAKING IT TO THE WORD

➤ **Read** Isaiah 33:15–16.

➤ Do you think Christians might have a different approach to Jen's dilemma than other people? Why or why not?

➤ What do these verses tell us about God, and how we should try to live our lives as his followers?

➤ Jen isn't accepting bribes, but how might these verses apply to her?

➤ What does this passage seem to suggest about people who treat others fairly?

B24

THEME: ## Lies and gossip

BIBLE: ## Ephesians 4

Lies about Lau

Lau had been working on her science project about volcanoes for two weeks. She'd done a lot of research on the Internet and she'd even got her dad to drive her to the library so she could learn more. Finally the day had arrived when her science class would be graded on their projects. Lau was a pretty good student; she wasn't at the top of her class but after all her hard work, she was hoping to get an excellent grade.

In class, her teacher, Mr Taunton, was writing the grades on the board. Lau scanned her eyes over her classmates' names, eager to see what grade she'd got for her volcano project. Lau saw that she'd got an A, her best grade in science yet. What's more, she'd got the highest score in her class.

She had worked hard and was delighted that it had all paid off. By now the whole class were talking about their grades; most of the other students had got a B or a C. That's when Lau noticed that some girls in the back of the class were staring and pointing at her.

At break-time, one of the girls from the back of the class came up to her. 'You cheated on that project,' the girl told Lau. 'I'm going to make sure everyone knows.'

Lau was horrified, angry and upset – she never cheated on tests. Now this girl was spreading a lie about her. What's more, Lau was sure the lie would get back to Mr Taunton and she was worried that the grade she'd worked so hard for would be taken away from her.

OPENING UP

➤ What would you do in Lau's situation?

➤ What do you think prompted the girl to lie about Lau?

➤ Do you think Lau should forgive the girl? Why or why not? If so, when?

➤ Has anyone told a lie about you? How did you feel?

DIGGING DEEPER

➤ Do you ever find yourself telling lies? In what kinds of situations might you do this?

➤ What kind of consequences have you seen in the long term when you or others have told a lie?

➤ Do you think there's such a thing as a 'white lie'? Where is the line between this and a 'bad' or 'real' lie?

➤ What might the positive and negative effects be if no one ever lied?

TAKING IT TO THE WORD

➤ **Read** Ephesians 4:17–32.

➤ Why does Paul say that Christians should live a certain way? What right does he have to expect this?

➤ What does this passage say about lies and gossip?

➤ How realistic do you think this passage is? Explain your answer.

➤ Pray together, that you'll receive God's help in seeking to live as 'children of light'.

B25

THEME: Friendship

BIBLE: John 15

Hannah's betrayal

Hannah and Jodie had been hanging out together for most of the summer and had planned to go to the last big party before school began again. Both Hannah's and Jodie's parents had given them permission to go to the party, but at the last minute Jodie's parents changed their minds and told her she had to stay at home.

Jodie begged Hannah to go to the party on her own. Jodie had been suffering from a serious crush all summer on Steve, a guy who was going to be there, and she wanted to ask him out before school started up again. Hannah agreed to go to the party and to tell Steve that Jodie liked him.

The big night arrived, and the girls spent an hour on the phone together planning what Hannah would say to Steve about Jodie. They had it all worked out when Hannah headed off to the party. When she arrived there, Steve headed straight over to talk to her. Steve seemed to remember that he'd met her and Jodie several times over the summer. This seemed like a good sign. As Steve recounted their meetings at the beach and the fair, though, it became obvious it wasn't Jodie he was interested in – it was Hannah.

Even though Hannah hadn't ever thought about Steve as a boyfriend before, she found him very attractive, and enjoyed the attention. As the evening went on, Hannah and Steve talked more, and Hannah's plan to tell Steve about Jodie just melted away.

When Hannah's parents came to pick her up from the party, Steve stopped her and asked for a kiss goodbye. Hannah agreed but afterwards she felt really guilty – she had betrayed her friend for a boy. When Hannah and Jodie saw each other the next day, Hannah couldn't bear to admit the truth, and told Jodie that Steve hadn't shown up. The girls were friends for now, but Hannah knew that Jodie would find out the truth when they returned to school.

OPENING UP

➤ What do you think of Hannah's behaviour? What might you have done in her position?

➤ How bad do you think Hannah's mistake is? Why?

➤ What do you think Hannah should do next? What do you think Jodie's reaction would be?

➤ If you were Jodie, would you forgive Hannah? Why or why not?

DIGGING DEEPER

➤ How much do you trust your friends? Are there some friends who are more likely to let you down than others? How do you choose who you can trust?

➤ Can any person be trusted completely? Why or why not? If not, should we trust anyone?

➤ Do you think you are a trustworthy person and friend? Why or why not?

TAKING IT TO THE WORD

➤ **Read** John 15:12–17.

➤ What do these verses tell us about our responsibility to our friends?

➤ How did Jesus' example raise the bar for friendship?

➤ Is it possible to love each other as much as God loves us? If not, what do you think this verse is really saying?

➤ What is the meaning of the word 'fruit' (verse 16)? What is 'fruit that will last'? What does that have to do with friend-ship?

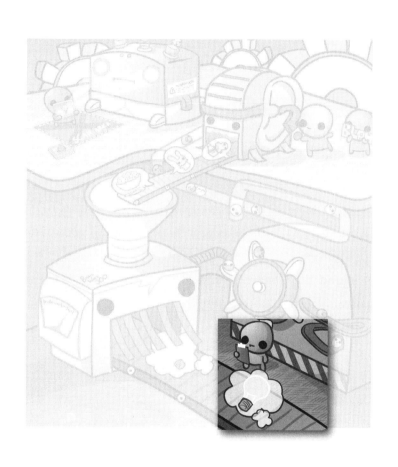

Section C
Famous Names

Introduction

We live in the age of celebrity. A cultural Frankenstein's monster, created by a mix of profit-hungry media bosses and wide-eyed sections of the public, the fame phenomenon is one of the defining features of Western society today.

Middle-of-the-road sportsmen are paid like kings, and looked up to as if they are even more than that. A teenage pop star sells one record by building up an Internet fan base, and suddenly he's being referred to as 'the next Elvis Presley'. Our television screens seem continually illuminated by wave after wave of so-called 'reality' shows and invasive documentaries, along the lines of 'Help, I look a bit like a monkey', which throw unsuspecting but fame-hungry people into the spotlight for a few moments. Suddenly, Mr Monkey-face is everywhere – promoting male grooming products and getting into a drunken fight at an airport.

Young people are constantly being asked to evaluate and make decisions on this stream of 'famous' people that passes in front of their eyes. Some they will decide are foolish, and not worth taking an interest in. Others will become their heroes, idols and pin-ups. Somewhere in the middle the bulk of celebrities remain, like guilty pleasures – young people want to know about them, and build up a huge bank of knowledge about their lives and activities, but don't let on.

If you want to put this theory to the test, simply hold a quiz night, and watch how the scores across the board rocket when you get to the 'obscure celebrities' round. Young people have a huge pop-culture data-base in their heads, and a large part of it is dominated by famous faces.

So what do we do with this as Christians and youth workers? We certainly don't agree with the idea of hero worship; nor are we fond of poking fun at those who have fallen from grace. However, if we don't engage at all with the celebrity culture, we're neglecting to listen to where young people are coming from. As Youth for Christ's 'Three Story Evangelism' model puts it, we're trying to tell them our story without listening to theirs.

Tragic as it might seem, the celebrity culture is part of young people's collective story. It's the society they were brought up in, and it's something they understand completely. So the stories of famous (or briefly famous) people become tools that help them to interpret the world around them.

Before that sounds too frightening, that doesn't mean that young people blindly copy their heroes. Some do, but the majority aren't that foolish. Instead, they use these stories to help them think through important (and less important) issues. If your favourite singer goes into rehab, you don't rush to join her, but you might begin to think through the consequences of drink and drugs.

That's where we come in – as youth workers it's part of our job to help young people to think about these issues, and to make wise and informed choices about them. The next set of twenty-five discussion starters is intended as a tool for this purpose. Each discussion takes a person who has featured in the news in recent years, and unpacks their story. Some of the names will be known to you, others may be less familiar; all have been included because something they have done is worth talking about.

C1

THEME: **Marriage**

BIBLE: **Ephesians 5**

Marriage on TV

Richard Madeley and Judy Finnegan married in 1986, when they were both beginning their careers in TV. Just two years into their marriage, the pair were offered the chance to present a new British daytime television programme called *This Morning*. The show was soon attracting a regular audience of two million viewers. During this time the couple also had their two children, Jack and Chloe.

Due to the popularity of the programme, it soon became evident that Richard and Judy had lost much of the privacy that married couples have in day-to-day life. The nation was watching their every move and many of their personal choices were scrutinized by the media.

When Judy took a break from the programme in 1997, the media spread rumours that the couple's marriage was on the rocks. After three months of speculation, Judy returned to the programme stating that health problems, not marriage problems, had kept her away.

Several years later Richard and Judy left *This Morning* to present a more relaxed afternoon show on another channel. Despite many incidents where their marriage and family decisions have been thrust into the media spotlight, their marriage has somehow continued unscathed. Today, Richard and Judy have enjoyed over twenty years of married life together.

OPENING UP

➤ Richard and Judy have the added pressure of millions of people knowing when their marriage is strong and when it is weak. Do you think the fame and pay-cheques they receive as part of their jobs make all that pressure worth it?

➤ Do you think celebrities should be allowed privacy or do they sacrifice that when they choose to become famous? What if they didn't decide to become famous?

➤ Imagine either that Richard and Judy are your parents, or that your parents host a daytime TV show. As their children, how do you feel about so many people watching them?

DIGGING DEEPER

➤ Despite media pressures, Richard and Judy have been married for over twenty years. What do you think makes a good marriage? What does marriage mean to you?

➤ Who is involved in a marriage? Is it just the husband and wife or are others involved?

➤ Think about wedding vows: what promises are often made between a husband and wife? What do they really mean? Do you think people take these vows seriously? Which ones are taken less seriously?

TAKING IT TO THE WORD

➤ **Read** Ephesians 5:25–33.

➤ What do you think it means to love your wife or husband as you love yourself?

➤ How do you think Christ loves the church?

➤ What else do we learn about marriage from this passage? How can we apply this teaching to other, non-married relationships, with one another and with God?

C2

THEME: # Growing up fast

BIBLE: # 1 Samuel 15

Too much too young?

At just 18 years of age, England footballer Wayne Rooney had the world, and not just the ball, at his feet. Fans in England and beyond believed he could grow into the greatest footballer in the country's history, while one team was standing by to pay almost £30 million to secure his services. So while Rooney had more money than he could spend and more natural ability than eleven of his contemporaries put together, he also learned from a young age that he would carry an enormous weight of expectation on his shoulders. England expects Wayne Rooney to mature into its saviour – and fast.

It's not unusual these days for players to come under such immense pressure at such a young age. Some, like David Beckham, handled it well, but others have not been so fortunate. Former Arsenal and Cardiff City winger Leon Jeanne found himself on a £1,000-a-week salary while he was still a teenager, but after falling in with the wrong crowd he became addicted to cocaine and was eventually sacked by his club. Within months he had appeared in court on drug-dealing charges. Stephen Hopkins QC, prosecuting, told the jury: 'In many ways you might have some sympathy for him. He found fame and fortune at a young age. Quite clearly he was overwhelmed.'

OPENING UP

➤ Why do you think it all went wrong for Leon Jeanne?

➤ What advice would you give to Wayne Rooney to help him avoid ending up like Leon?

➤ How do you think you'd deal with having intense pressure and a megabucks salary thrust upon you right now?

DIGGING DEEPER

➤ What are your ambitions right now? How highly do money and fame feature among your hopes and dreams?

➤ Why do you think the ideals of fame and fortune are so important to young people today?

➤ If only a few people can actually be rich or famous, what does this mean for the majority who aim for this but miss out?

TAKING IT TO THE WORD

➤ **Read** 1 Samuel 15:1–29 (or summarize verses 1–23, and read just verses 24–29).

➤ Saul was a gifted king, but he didn't have a strong character to back up his gifts, and in the end God punished him. How should he have acted differently?

➤ Why do you think God chose to punish Saul?

➤ What are the pitfalls of being gifted – and of misusing that gift?

➤ Get into pairs – be honest with and encourage each other. Discuss: what gifts do you think you have? Which do you think your partner has? Which gifts would you like?

➤ Pray together, asking God to give you gifts, but also the strong characters that you'll need to make the best use of them.

C3

THEME: **God's deal**

BIBLE: **John 3**

A paper clip for a house

Among the thousands of net-heads who've tried to make a fast buck from the Internet with little effort and a clever idea, Canadian Kyle MacDonald stands out. Instead of selling web-page pixels at inflated rates, or offering the secrets of a better life for a ten-dollar fee, Kyle's big Internet idea is all about silliness and fun. However, it might well net him a fortune in the process.

In 2005, Kyle set out on a ridiculous mission – to swap one red paperclip for a house. Of course, he wasn't expecting to find a person willing to make that trade, but through a series of smaller swaps, he wondered if he could get there eventually. And so far, it's going pretty well.

After posting the idea on his website, Kyle got an offer for his paperclip – a fish-shaped pen. He agreed, and soon swapped the pen for a doorknob. A few trades later, he'd worked his way up to a snowmobile, then a recording contract. A year into his quest, he'd managed to trade that for a year's rent-free accommodation in Arizona. But Kyle told reporters he wouldn't stop trading until he achieved his goal, claiming: 'I'm going to keep trading for bigger or better things until I get a house.'

OPENING UP

➤ Do you think Kyle will eventually reach his goal? Why or why not?

➤ What possession, idea or person would you give up a house for?

➤ Is there anything big or important enough that you'd change your whole life in order to get it?

DIGGING DEEPER

➤ If someone you didn't know asked you to sell them something for much less than it was worth, would you consider it? Why or why not?

➤ Do you think good deeds deserve something in return? Why or why not? If so, what should be received?

TAKING IT TO THE WORD

➤ **Read** John 3:12–20.

➤ Jesus is explaining God's great swap deal to Nicodemus. How is there an exchange in verse 16? What is God asking for?

➤ What do you think is a bigger swap – a house for a paperclip, or eternal life for a decision to believe in and follow someone? Why?

➤ Do you think God is asking for a lot in return for eternal life? Explain your answer.

➤ Read 2 Corinthians 5:21 – Jesus' death is exchanged for life for everyone. Is it a fair swap? How does Jesus' sacrifice here make you feel? How do you respond?

C4

THEME: **Prayer/staying in touch**

BIBLE: **Matthew 6**

ur dad cares bout u

Teens are not renowned for keeping in constant communication with their parents. Yet in an increasingly dangerous world, many parents are concerned that they often don't know the whereabouts of their offspring. In an effort to address this issue, Maths teacher Sally Dowler, whose daughter Milly was abducted and murdered on her way home from school, came up with an answer. She and her husband launched the 'Teach UR Mum 2 TXT' campaign, an attempt to encourage adults to engage with shorthand text messaging – the language used by young people everywhere.

As a result of the initiative, young people throughout the UK received a free booklet designed to help them to explain text messaging to their parents, and listing a number of helpful phrases. These included 'ruok' ('Are you OK?'), 'cul8r' ('See you later') and 'tmb' ('Text me back'). Sally's other daughter, Gemma, wrote in the booklet: 'Having seen how awful it was 4 my parents wen my sister Milly went missing, I now know how important it is 2 let ur parents know where u r @ all times. It's much less embarrassing 2 get a txt than a fone call.'

OPENING UP

➤ Do you use text messaging to contact your parents/guardians? Do you think it's a good idea to encourage young people to do this? Why or why not?

➤ Do you text friends? Why – to convey information or just to keep in touch?

➤ What other kinds of communication do you use, and for what purposes?

➤ What happens to relationships when you don't keep in touch?

DIGGING DEEPER

➤ Should teenagers keep someone informed about their whereabouts at all times, or some of the time… or is it no one else's business?

➤ Why might some teenagers not want their parents to know where they are?

➤ What's more important (with particular reference to this story) – personal safety or personal freedom?

TAKING IT TO THE WORD

➤ **Read** Matthew 6:5–15.

➤ What do we learn about prayer in this passage? Are there some good guidelines here for us?

➤ If prayer is about keeping in touch with God, what happens if we don't pray?

➤ How much time do you spend praying, compared to talking, emailing or texting? Do you think that's a good balance? This week, try to spend more time keeping in touch with your parents, on earth and in heaven.

C5

THEME: **God's plan**

BIBLE: **Job 1**

The bigger picture

Gordon Ramsey had dreamed of becoming a professional football player throughout his childhood. And when, during a match for his youth team, he was spotted by a Glasgow Rangers scout, it seemed all his dreams had come true.

After completing trials, Gordon was signed up by Rangers, aged 15. For three years, he played for the youth teams of a club which was consistently at the top of the Scottish championship. It was one of the best teams in Europe for a young player to learn his trade in. There was a problem, however. One of Gordon's knees was consistently giving him problems, and he often missed matches through injury. Eventually, doctors told Gordon that his knee wasn't healing properly. His professional football career was over before it had really begun.

Most people are planning their first career when they turn 18, but Gordon was already faced with the reality that he would have to embark on a second one. Devastated, he had to rethink his entire future.

After careful thought, he began his second career as

a chef, a decision that saw him leave his hometown in Scotland to study in London and Paris with some of the best chefs in the world. Thanks to his determination and hard work, Gordon is now a TV celebrity chef, with restaurants in London, Tokyo and New York. He still occasionally plays a game of football for charity, but it seems strange to think that, had it not been for a sad and heart-breaking problem, Gordon's true gifting might never have come to the surface.

OPENING UP

➤ Imagine you are in the position Gordon found himself in when he found out he would never be able to play football again. How would you feel?

➤ Looking back now, do you think Gordon would be able to see the 'bigger picture' and not feel angry about having to give up football?

➤ What do you think Gordon learnt from his first career as a footballer and his injury?

DIGGING DEEPER

➤ Do you think God has a plan for us? Does this include our careers?

➤ Think of a time when you have had to give up something you love doing temporarily or permanently. Was it hard? Why?

➤ Consider the last time you were angry. Were you angry at yourself, your family and friends, or even God? How did you recover? What did you learn?

➤ Think about two very different things that you are good at. How would you feel to lose one of these skills?

TAKING IT TO THE WORD

➤ **Read** Job 1:1–22.

> ➤ Despite terrible things happening to Job, he doesn't give up on God – is this how a Christian should act when bad things happen?
>
> ➤ You may have heard the phrase, 'the Lord giveth and the Lord taketh away' before. What do you think it means?
>
> ➤ How do you think Job's story compares to Gordon's?

C6
THEME: **Changing direction**
BIBLE: **Luke 19**

Jack's change of course

In 2003, 18-year-old Jack Osbourne was becoming even more notorious than his infamous rocker dad Ozzy. Seriously overweight, with a severe drink problem and an addiction to the drug OxyContin, Jack was in danger of throwing his life away, both because and in spite of his growing fame as a reality TV star.

Then one day, Jack took a look around at the collection of heroin addicts and hard drinkers who had become his crew – all of them older than him – and realized that he didn't want to end up like that. He checked himself into a rehab clinic, where he spent two months detoxing and in intense individual and group therapy. Enrolling in an Alcoholics Anonymous programme, he chose 'nature' as his inspirational 'higher power'.

Four years on, Jack was five stone lighter, and both drug- and drink-free. The time in rehab both solved his short-term crises and inspired him to aim for new and different things. He became, as the name of his television show suggests, *Jack Osbourne: Adrenaline Junkie*, replacing the drink and drug highs with those offered by base-jumping and extreme rock-climbing. In doing so, he confounded the cynics who believed that he would burn out at age 20, and became a dramatically different kind of celebrity role model.

OPENING UP

➤ Jack's life took a dramatic change of direction. What events led to it?

➤ How do you think Jack viewed his life before rehab? And what about now?

➤ Can you think of other examples of people who've made dramatic changes of direction? Why did they change course?

DIGGING DEEPER

➤ Why do you think many famous people end up in rehab? What is it about the celebrity lifestyle which leads them there?

➤ Do you think you'd be able to avoid that sort of pitfall if you were rich and famous? Why or why not? How would you try?

TAKING IT TO THE WORD

➤ **Read** Luke 19:1–10.

➤ Describe Zacchaeus' dramatic change of life direction. How is it similar to Jack Osbourne's? How is it different?

➤ How do you think Zacchaeus' life change impacted on those around him? What about Jack?

➤ Can you think of a point at which your life changed direction? If so, describe it. If not, do you want to change course? How?

C7
THEME: **Racism**
BIBLE: **Mark 7**

Racist Ron?

'Big' Ron Atkinson was one of England's best-loved football commentators. An often nonsensical perma-tanned 60-something who seemed to have sunbathed himself into a permanent state of verbal diarrhoea, he could always be relied upon to liven up a dull match with a bizarre turn of phrase that had fans rolling in their armchairs. Quite what 'a lightning slow striker', 'offering the curly finger', 'a Hollywood ball' or 'little eyebrows' are, perhaps only Ron will ever know.

But Big Ron fell gracelessly from his plinth when commentating on a big game involving Chelsea. During a commercial break, Ron referred to Chelsea's Marcel Desailly (a player of African descent) as 'a f***ing lazy n*****' in a conversation with an ITV colleague. And while no one in England could hear it, Ron was unaware that his remark was accidentally being broadcast to Arabic countries using ITV's sound and video feed. Ron immediately resigned from his position, saying: 'I can't believe I did it. It was just a moment of stupidity.'

OPENING UP

➤ What do you think Ron's punishment should have been? Why?

➤ Do you think he should ever be allowed to pick up the microphone again? Why or why not?

➤ After this happened, Ron said he was not a racist, and that the comment just 'slipped out'. Does that change anything? Why?

➤ If Ron had managed to bite his tongue, would he still have been fired? Why?

DIGGING DEEPER

➤ Do you think racism still really exists in your local area? Why or why not? Are you aware of any changes in the levels of racism in recent years?

➤ What factors do you think make racism get worse or better in a community?

➤ Why do you think people express racist attitudes? How can you ensure that you don't?

TAKING IT TO THE WORD

➤ **Read** Mark 7:1–23.

➤ What is Jesus saying in this passage? Why did he need to say it?

➤ What's more important – what we say, or what we think?

➤ What does Big Ron need to do – apologize, stop saying racist remarks, or something else?

➤ Pray for one another, that God will change your attitudes from the inside.

C8

THEME: **Friendship**

BIBLE: **1 Samuel 20**

I'll be there for you...

After ten series, spanning nearly as many years, the six New Yorkers from TV's *Friends* finally went their separate ways. For all of that time, they remained top of the television ratings tree – with ad spots during the finale episode selling at a staggering two million dollars per minute. Most agree that the show will go down as a comedy classic, but while Ross, Rachel and co. made a generation laugh, they also defined the spirit of their age. They placed friendship above all else – even above family – at a time when the real world was doing the same. In the 1960s and 70s, the most popular television programmes were family-centred soap operas. By the 1990s, stories of friendship had become king.

Although over the course of nearly 250 episodes, some of the relationships between the friends had their ups and downs, in the end they remained firmly connected to one another. All of the friendships stood the test of time – and while some think the show was all about sex, money and selfishness, its true message was summed up in the words of the title song: 'I'll be there for you, 'cause you're there for me too.'

OPENING UP

> What defines a true friend?

> What would you do for friendship, even if there was nothing for yourself to gain? Why?

> Who has been a good friend to you? What made them a good friend?

DIGGING DEEPER

> What kind of friend are you? Do you treat some friends better than others?

> How good is the quality of your conversations with friends? Do you ask your friends open questions, or mainly yes/no stuff? Do you talk about things that matter, or just sport and TV?

TAKING IT TO THE WORD

> **Read** 1 Samuel 20:16–17.

> How strong was Jonathan and David's friendship? How do we know?

> How do you think we should view friendship in the light of this?

> Make a list of things you could do to be a better friend. Pray for God's help, and then try to do some of them this week.

C9

THEME: **Self-image**

BIBLE: **Genesis 1/1 Peter 3**

Reducing Kate

Kate Winslet started acting when she was just 11 years old and went on to get her first major film role at 17. Over the next five years she became a world-famous actress and soon found she was able to pick and choose the kinds of roles she wanted to play.

Throughout her career Kate has often chosen to turn down lead roles in big Hollywood films so she can play strong, confident women – the kind of characters more suited to her own personality. Off screen, Kate is very keen to be a positive role model for girls, including her own daughter, Mia.

One issue she feels passionately about is promoting a positive body image to all women and girls. In recent years, Kate has become known for refusing to diet in order to conform to Hollywood ideals of increasingly skinny women. When, in 2003, a popular magazine digitally modified photographs of Kate to make her appear drastically thinner than she was, the actress was horrified by the results and publicly denied giving her consent to the changes.

OPENING UP

➤ How do you think Kate Winslet felt when she saw images of herself made to look drastically thinner?

➤ Was it right for the magazine to change Kate's appearance? Why?

➤ Who is responsible for promoting a positive body image? The press? Celebrities? Family and friends? Why?

DIGGING DEEPER

➤ How important is physical appearance?

➤ What makes someone beautiful? Is it always something physical?

➤ Have you ever wanted to change something about the way you look? If so, what and why?

TAKING IT TO THE WORD

➤ **Read** Genesis 1:27 and then 1 Peter 3:3–4.

➤ What do you think it means to be 'created in God's image'?

➤ Is 'beauty of spirit' the same as physical beauty?

➤ Think again about what makes a person beautiful. Has your view changed from before? How?

C10
THEME: Defining moments
BIBLE: Acts 8

Sophie's moment

Like most members of her profession, actress Sophie Okonedo had spent years going from job to job, mainly playing small parts in TV dramas. She had never believed that superstardom was possible for her, and had resigned herself to remaining what she called 'a jobbing British actress' for the whole of her career. Not for her the roles in *Star Wars* or *Harry Potter* – instead she took her place in the cast of *Hotel Rwanda*, a small-time film starring mainly unknowns.

But then, one moment changed everything for Sophie. After completing work on the film, she was at an art gallery with her mother when she received a phone call from her publicist. 'She was croaking – she could barely get the words out,' Sophie recalls. Sophie had been nominated for an Oscar – the most prestigious acting award of all – for her performance in *Hotel Rwanda*.

Sophie and her mum celebrated so exuberantly, they were thrown out of the gallery. It didn't matter. She didn't win the Oscar – that didn't matter either. Once the jobbing actress, Sophie has now taken her place in

Hollywood's elite. 'It's amazing how suddenly your world can turn around,' she says. 'At 1.29 p.m. on that day, my life was one-way – ordinary, predictable. By 1.32, it was unrecognizable.'

OPENING UP

➤ How might Sophie Okonedo have felt before, during and after that phone call?

➤ What would be the equivalent phone call for you?

➤ What experience have you had of a single moment massively changing your life?

DIGGING DEEPER

➤ How prepared are you for sudden change? Do you fear change, or does it excite you?

➤ Do you feel you keep your eyes and ears open to new opportunities? Why or why not?

➤ What one change – which is out of your hands – would you love to see happen to your life? Why?

TAKING IT TO THE WORD

➤ **Read** Acts 8:26–39.

➤ What are the similarities between this story and Sophie's?

➤ How do you think the Ethiopian felt before, during and after this revolutionary moment?

➤ How might we be involved in similar moments, either in Philip's role, or that of the Ethiopian? How do we prepare for these moments?

➤ Pray for one another, that God will equip you for revolutionary moments, and lead you to and through them.

C11

THEME: **Charity**

BIBLE: **Malachi 3**

Giving his all?

Bill Gates, the founder of the world's largest software company, Microsoft, is considered to be the richest person in the world. His personal fortune is £27 billion and is growing daily. Bill and his wife Melinda own one of the most expensive houses in the world.

In 2000, Bill started the Bill and Melinda Gates foundation, a charity that would fund college scholarships for underprivileged students and research to find a vaccine for AIDS and diseases found in third-world countries.

To start his charity, Bill invested £54 million, around 2 per cent of his entire fortune. The charity is still very successful today and is said to have encouraged other billionaires to give large amounts of their fortunes to charities.

OPENING UP

➤ Bill Gates is currently the richest man in the world. He has given 2 per cent of his fortune to charity. Should he give more? Why?

➤ If you were Bill Gates for the day, how would you spend your money? How soon would you think about charities?

DIGGING DEEPER

➤ Name some charities. Which are most important to you, and why?

➤ Does charity always mean offering money? How else can you be charitable?

➤ Think about your daily life – school, friends, family. What was the last act of charity you remember seeing? What was the last act of charity that you were involved in? What happened, and what were the results?

TAKING IT TO THE WORD

➤ **Read** Malachi 3:10–12.

➤ Why do you think this concept of tithing is important to Christians?

➤ Is tithing relevant today? If yes, should everyone do it? It refers to the idea of a tenth of a person's wealth. Do you think we should give away exactly 10 per cent? Why or why not?

➤ Do you think the idea of tithing and giving is only for adults and full-time earners? Why or why not?

➤ Giving is mentioned frequently in the Bible. Why do you think it's such an important issue? How might you need to reconsider the idea of giving?

C12

THEME: **Acting justly**

BIBLE: **Nehemiah 5**

Do the right thing

Footballer Mauricio Taricco was nearing the end of his career. No longer wanted by his club, Tottenham Hotspur, who had bought a new, younger player for his position, he began to wonder whether he'd kicked his last ball. So when the phone rang, and another team, West Ham United, asked if he'd like to come and play for them instead, Taricco was overjoyed to realize that his career was not yet over. He travelled quickly to the club, signed on the dotted line, and guaranteed himself another season of football and another year of hefty pay cheques.

His experience meant that he went straight into the first team, and lined up for his first match just two days later. But just half an hour into the game, he felt a muscle in his leg give way, and found himself in agony on the floor, certain to be out with injury for six weeks or more. Taricco had always had a bad reputation in the football world. His aggressive style had earned him few friends, but quite a few red and yellow cards over the years. So what happened next surprised many. Instead of spending the next two months draining West Ham's finances while sitting on the sidelines, Taricco himself decided to terminate his contract, denying himself a six-figure sum in wages. 'I came here to solve a problem, not to give them another one,' he told the startled media.

OPENING UP

➤ Why do you think Taricco decided to terminate his contract?

➤ What do you think this decision will do to his bad reputation?

➤ What would you have done in his position? Why?

DIGGING DEEPER

➤ Do you believe in doing the right thing? Why or why not? Are there some times or places when you're more likely to do the right thing?

➤ What does it actually mean to 'do the right thing'? Who says what's right or wrong?

TAKING IT TO THE WORD

➤ **Read** Nehemiah 5:14–18.

➤ What are the similarities between this story and Taricco's?

➤ Why did Nehemiah act in this way? What might the lesson be here for us?

➤ Are there times when you might choose to lay aside your 'rights' for the benefit of the community or youth group?

➤ Pray together, that you'll always do the right thing, even when it might be to your own cost.

C13

THEME: **Generosity**

BIBLE: **2 Corinthians 9**

Cash from Keanu

When Warner Brothers decided to film two sequels to the hit movie *The Matrix*, they knew how important it was to persuade the cast of the first film to appear again. In fact, they thought it was so important that they offered leading man Keanu Reeves the biggest deal in Hollywood's history. Understandably, Reeves agreed, but not before negotiating a contract clause which netted him 15 per cent of box-office takings for both *The Matrix Reloaded* and its follow-up *The Matrix Revolutions*. Conservative estimates put his likely earnings from that agreement at around £70 million.

Many people in Reeves' position would have been eyeing up small Caribbean islands or booking a place on the next Russian space flight. Incredibly, though, the man who played Neo decided to give at least £50 million away, donating it to poorly paid effects and costume designers who had worked on the *Matrix* trilogy. When asked about his decision by incredulous journalists, Reeves answered: 'Money is the last thing I think about. I could live on what I've already made for the next few centuries.'

OPENING UP

➤ If you were given £70 million, what would you do with it? Try to be completely honest.

➤ Why do you think Keanu Reeves decided to give so much money away? What do you think he will receive in return?

➤ How would the world be different if everyone displayed this attitude?

DIGGING DEEPER

➤ What would you say was your view of money? Do you wish you had more? Do you wish you spent less?

➤ How does it feel when you give money away? Would you like to do this more? If so, what stops you?

TAKING IT TO THE WORD

➤ **Read** 2 Corinthians 9:6–8.

➤ Why should Christians give money away?

➤ Should you give in order to receive something? (Check Matthew 6:1–4 if you are unsure.)

➤ It doesn't seem that Keanu gave his money away 'under compulsion'. Do you ever give reluctantly?

➤ What other things, aside from money, can you give away for God?

➤ Think about all the people who'll benefit from Keanu Reeves' generosity. What kinds of people could benefit from yours?

➤ Think about your finances. Should you be giving more away? Pray that God will help you to become a 'cheerful' giver.

C14

THEME: **Second chances**

BIBLE: **Acts 15/2 Timothy 4**

Changing fortunes

TV make-over maestro Laurence Llewelyn-Bowen thought he'd gambled away nearly half a million pounds of charity money – until a big-hearted TV company decided to give him a second chance.

The flamboyant presenter was taking part in a special celebrity edition of the TV quiz show *Who Wants to Be a Millionaire?*, when things started to go rather well. Before long, Laurence and his wife Jackie had become the first celebrities ever to face the rare £1 million jackpot question. They were asked: 'Translated from the Latin, what is the motto of the United States?'

Confident from his success so far, Laurence answered, 'In God we Trust.' However, host Chris Tarrant informed him that the answer was in fact, 'One out of Many.' A devastated Laurence saw his winnings – earmarked for a children's hospice – plummet to just £32,000.

But while the answer was technically incorrect, Celador, the makers of the show, decided after the show that their question was too ambiguous, as both the answers are mottoes of the US. They agreed to invite Laurence back for a shot at another £1 million question, and since he and his wife had no idea of the correct answer, this time they refused to gamble and took away £500,000 for their charity.

'We feel as if we've been reprieved from the firing squad,' he said afterwards. 'How unusual is it to get a second chance in life?'

OPENING UP

➤ How do you think Laurence felt when he realized he'd lost? And how about when he heard of his reprieve?

➤ What's the answer to Laurence's question – 'How unusual is it to get a second chance in life?' Why?

➤ Share with a partner a situation in which you wish you had a second chance. Now share a situation in which you have the power to give someone else a reprieve.

DIGGING DEEPER

➤ What kinds of wrongs do you find it easiest to forgive? Which kinds of mistakes are hardest to forgive?

➤ Do you believe that people should always pay for their mistakes? In what circumstances might people be let off?

➤ Do you believe in capital punishment (the death sentence)? Why?

TAKING IT TO THE WORD

➤ **Read** Acts 15:36–41 and 2 Timothy 4:11.

➤ How does Paul's attitude to Mark change over the years? What must have happened in Paul, and in this relationship, between the two writings?

➤ How can you follow Paul's example here in your own life? Pray together, that God will show you where to reconcile, forgive, and give second chances.

C15
THEME: Imposed religion

BIBLE: Romans 12/Matthew 26

Catho-land

Businessman Tom Monaghan has a dream. Tom longs to live in a world that isn't as dark and murky as the one we see around us today. He thinks pornography and freely available contraception are the architects of our society's downfall. He wishes he could live in a place where both are banned – but no such place exists, at least not in America.

So he's building his own town.

That's right – Domino's Pizza founder and billionaire Tom is spending $400 million of his personal fortune on constructing Ave Maria, a new community in Florida. It'll be governed on strict Catholic lines, with no pornography, no condoms or birth-control pills, and a ban on X-rated television channels. And while civil liberties groups have reacted with outrage, Tom's vision could soon be realized – there have already been 7,000 enquiries about the 11,000 homes that are being built there.

OPENING UP

➤ What do think it would be like to live in Ave Maria? Would you like to live there? Why or why not?

➤ Tom's town will have a heavy religious focus, with many churches, including a large cathedral at the centre. Do you think he should impose his religion in this way? Or is he just reflecting the world as God intended it?

➤ How do you think the town might change over time?

DIGGING DEEPER

➤ Do you think it's ever acceptable for people to impose their religion on non-followers? If so, in what circumstances?

➤ Have you ever felt that others imposed their beliefs on you? If so, what happened?

➤ Leaving religion to one side – how else do you feel people or institutions force their opinions on you or others?

TAKING IT TO THE WORD

➤ **Read** Romans 12:1–2 and Matthew 26:6–13.

➤ These verses from Romans might be the kind of passage Tom would quote to support his plan. Do you think this would be a fair claim, based on these verses?

➤ Would moving to a town like Ave Maria help you to 'be transformed'?

➤ In Matthew 26, the implication is that this woman was a 'bad' woman, possibly a prostitute – why was the Son of God so positive about her?

➤ What kind of challenge does Jesus' own example present to a potential Ave Maria resident?

C16

THEME: **Power**

BIBLE: **2 Samuel 5**

Shaping the world

In 2000, politician Al Gore was running against George W. Bush for the position of President of the United States. After a very close election where counting the final vote took nearly a month, it was announced that Al Gore had lost the election and Bush would be President.

Having lost the opportunity to the most influential man in the world, Al decided to leave politics and focus on another task, one he considered just as important as being President of the United States.

Al chose to turn all his attention to a problem that had concerned him since the 1970s – climate change. No longer working as a politician and confident that he could teach the public about the dangers of global warming, Al began touring the United States giving lectures to students, businesses and anyone who would listen.

In 2006 Al's lecture on climate change was made into the feature film documentary, *An Inconvenient Truth*. The film won numerous awards and helped hundreds of thousands of people around the world to understand the environmental threat of carbon emissions and global warming. Even though he wasn't President, he had still changed the world for the better.

Impressed by his work, many American politicians have suggested that Al should run for President of the United States again. Al, however, has insisted he would rather continue fighting the negative effects of climate change.

OPENING UP

➤ Who do you think has more influence – a politician or a filmmaker?

➤ Do you need to be in power to change things for the better? Why or why not?

➤ How do you think Al Gore felt when he lost the Presidential election? What about when *An Inconvenient Truth* began showing in cinemas?

DIGGING DEEPER

➤ Al Gore 'changed the world' through his documentary. How can we change the world for the better?

➤ What makes a good President? Is it the same things as a good leader?

➤ If you could do one thing to change the world for the better, what would you do?

TAKING IT TO THE WORD

➤ **Read** 2 Samuel 5.

> ➤ 2 Samuel recalls David's rise to power as king of Israel. Why does God give David this power and influence?

> ➤ What do you know about David's whole life story? With God's support, how many times did he change the world around him? Was he 'in power' during all those times?

> ➤ David and Al Gore both changed the world from a position of power; we also know that through God remarkable acts of change occurred before David was king. Do you think this means you don't need to be powerful to change the world?

> ➤ What do you think is a good definition of the word 'power'?

C17
THEME: **Ethics**
BIBLE: **Genesis 2**

Selling up or selling out?

In 1970, businesswoman Anita Roddick opened a single cosmetics shop to help support herself and her two children while her husband was travelling in America. This cosmetics shop wasn't going to be like all the others on the high street, though. Anita believed that a business could make a profit at the same time as making a positive contribution to the community.

Her business, called The Body Shop, grew quickly to several stores. It was one of the first chains of cosmetic shops to actively oppose animal testing and support fair trade. Over the course of three decades, her small business grew into a multi-million-pound empire.

In 2006, Anita decided to sell The Body Shop and announced she would be giving away half her fortune – a massive £51 million – to charity. While impressed at her generosity, fans of the eco-friendly shop were shocked to discover that the chain would be sold to a large company with alleged involvement in animal testing and other activities that Anita opposed.

OPENING UP

➤ Do you think Anita was right to sell The Body Shop to a company that perhaps doesn't follow the same ethical guidelines she does?

➤ Does her decision to give away half her fortune cancel out her choice to sell to a company with different ethical beliefs?

➤ Does it matter to you if the owners of The Body Shop or other stores test on animals? Would it stop you shopping there if they did?

DIGGING DEEPER

➤ Do you think companies should be required by law to tell the public if they test on animals? What effect would this law have on different kinds of businesses?

➤ Think about animal testing. Is it ever right? Does it matter what the tests are for – cosmetics or a cure for cancer?

➤ Would you be willing to work for a company that tests on animals?

➤ Think about all your possessions and any savings you might have. Do you think you could give half of your 'fortune' away to charity? Why?

TAKING IT TO THE WORD

➤ **Read** Genesis 2:19–20.

➤ What do these verses tell us about man's relationship to the animal kingdom?

➤ Do you think these verses condone animal testing or animal cruelty?

➤ What other passages in the Bible can you think of where animals are mentioned? How are they treated?

C18
THEME: Giving thanks
BIBLE: 2 Samuel 6

A unique thank-you

When the founder of Virgin, Richard Branson, bought a small island off the coast of Australia, most people thought it was the sort of luxury purchase that billionaires are famous for. Branson had big plans for his little island and began investing over £2 million in a leisure complex and sports facilities.

When the island had been fitted with tree-house accommodation, tennis courts and an area for water-skiing and sailing, Branson announced that in fact, Makepeace Island would be a luxury resort exclusively for the staff of Virgin worldwide.

Thanking his staff, Branson said Makepeace Island would be 'a wonderful retreat for them' and 'a great way for our team to spend time together and to get to know each other outside of a work environment'. Everyone had assumed that he was involved in a selfish project – in fact he was doing it all for others. He felt that his staff had done so much for him – he wanted to thank them in an extravagant manner that not only repaid their hard work, but symbolized the strength of his feeling.

OPENING UP

➤ Why do you think Richard Branson decided to invest so much money in a holiday resort for his staff?

➤ Would it have been better for him to just give his staff the money he spent on the island? Why or why not?

➤ If you worked for Richard Branson, how would you feel to find out you could have a free holiday on Makepeace Island? Might it encourage you to stay with his company?

DIGGING DEEPER

➤ By giving his employees free holidays, Richard Branson was able to offer them an experience they might not have been able to have otherwise. In what ways can we do this through our own giving?

➤ Consider your own friends and family. What non-material gifts would they like to receive most? Time? Relaxation? Support?

➤ Think about the ways you show your thanks to your loved ones and to God. How are they different?

TAKING IT TO THE WORD

➤ **Read** 2 Samuel 6:12–16.

➤ David's 'linen ephod' would have been quite revealing. What do you think about the fact that a king humbled himself in such a way, and showed such a disregard for how he was seen by others?

➤ How does this scene compare with how we worship today? What can we learn?

➤ Why do you think David behaved in this way?

➤ Who do you identify more with here – dancing David or his embarrassed wife?

C19

THEME: **Equality**
BIBLE: **Galatians 3**

Prisoner to President

The whole world was watching when, in 1990, Nelson Mandela was released from prison after serving twenty-seven years of a lifetime sentence. He had been charged with treason for disagreeing (sometimes violently) with the South African government's laws on apartheid, a system that classified citizens into racial groups and prioritized the rights and needs of white South Africans above all others.

Under these laws, hospitals and schools were divided by racial groups, with non-white citizens receiving inferior public services to whites. Non-white South Africans could no longer vote or have a passport.

During his years in prison, Mandela became one of the most well-known figures in the struggle against apartheid. Upon his release in 1990, the year apartheid was abolished, he knew that the battle was far from over, and began working on his political career.

Four years after his release, South Africa held the first election where politicians of all races could enter. Nelson Mandela won the vote and became the country's first black President in the process.

OPENING UP

➤ Nelson Mandela was kept in prison for twenty-seven years. Much of that time he was left in isolation. How do you think that tested his faith in his cause?

➤ In the Bible, Paul is also in prison because of his beliefs. What similarities are there between his trials and Nelson Mandela's?

➤ Mandela went from being in prison to being President in the space of four years. How do you think life would have changed for him in this time?

DIGGING DEEPER

➤ Think carefully about your own beliefs. Which are important to you? Are there any you would be willing to go to prison for? Try to be as honest as you can.

➤ Have you ever felt judged because of your race, religion or gender? How did you feel?

➤ Have you ever judged someone else because of their race, religion or gender? What kinds of judgments might you make about them? How do you feel about this?

TAKING IT TO THE WORD

➤ **Read** Galatians 3:26–29.

➤ In Galatians Jesus tells us we are all equal, and all welcome to follow God. As a Christian, do you feel equal to others?

➤ As Christians, we should welcome others and make them feel equal. What are some ways of doing that?

➤ What do you think it means to 'belong to Christ'?

C20
THEME: **Capital punishment**
BIBLE: **1 John 1 – 2**

A just killing?

Few would argue that Saddam Hussein's name will go down in history alongside those of the worst tyrants and dictators. He oppressed the people of Iraq for many years, indiscriminately murdering innocent villagers and turning a blind eye to injustice across the land. He invaded his neighbours, made enemies across the globe, and allegedly funded and supported terrorism against the West. Feared by his people, he enjoyed a life of palatial luxury while many of his subjects suffered in poverty. Put simply, he was not a good man.

During the second Iraq war, when Allied troops toppled him from rule, Saddam escaped to Tikrit, the town of his birth. In December 2003, he was discovered by US troops, cowering in a humble underground chamber. Dishevelled and unkempt, he looked a pathetic figure as he was presented to the world. His sons had been killed in a raid by US troops, and his rule had been forcibly ended. Squinting in the spotlight, he looked like a man with nothing left.

After a year-long trial in Iraq, Saddam's own people found him guilty of a string of charges, and pronounced a sentence that was perhaps inevitable. He was to receive the death penalty.

Fifty-six days later, Saddam was dead. Hung at dawn, he suffered a final indignity when his captors filmed footage of his death on their mobile phones. Inevitably, this soon found its way around the Internet. His execution took place on specially constructed gallows at a compound that had once been his military headquarters. The symbolism was not subtle, nor was it particularly tasteful.

Iraq's hated ex-leader was dead, and for many, justice had been done. Others were left wondering exactly what had been achieved through what amounted to murdering a mass-murderer.

OPENING UP

➤ What do you think of when you hear the name Saddam Hussein?

➤ Do you think Allied troops should have become involved in a war in Iraq? What are your views on the war?

➤ Do you think Saddam deserved to die for his crimes? Why or why not?

➤ Do you think the death penalty was the harshest sentence Saddam could have received? How else might he have been punished?

➤ Do you think Jesus would agree with Saddam's sentence? Why or why not?

DIGGING DEEPER

➤ Do you believe the death penalty is a good or bad idea? Why? If you agree with it, in what circumstances should it be used?

➤ Do you think capital punishment (the death penalty) prevents people from committing crimes? Why or why not?

➤ How does capital punishment theoretically deliver justice? Who is benefited, and how? In practice, does it achieve its purposes?

TAKING IT TO THE WORD

➤ **Read** 1 John 1:5 – 2:2.

➤ Do you think that Saddam Hussein was a 'worse' person than you are? Why? What about in the eyes of God?

➤ Does Jesus' offer of salvation (verse 7) extend to someone like Saddam Hussein? Why or why not?

➤ What does this passage teach us about ourselves and the nature of our sin?

➤ How might we respond to this passage in the way we live our lives?

C21
THEME: Perseverance
BIBLE: James 1

Down but not out

Stephen Hawking is perhaps the most respected scientist of the past few decades. His work, including the book *A Brief History of Time*, has both contributed hugely to his field of physics, and aroused the interest of millions of people around the world, eager to learn from his genius.

Yet while his brain is among the finest to ever grace the earth, his body is almost completely incapacitated. He suffers from an extraordinarily difficult illness called Motor Neuron Disease, which means that his daily life is a constant struggle. He is unable to speak, can barely move his body, and spends all his waking hours restricted to a wheelchair, with round-the-clock care a necessity.

Many sufferers of Motor Neuron Disease don't give up on their lives, but Stephen has gone to extraordinary lengths to prove that the illness has not beaten him. The computer system which is attached to his wheelchair recognizes small movements of his right cheek, with which, incredibly, he is able to compose speeches and research papers, and even browse the Internet. He continues to contribute to the scientific world, and regularly gives addresses to thousands of people through an electronic voice synthesizer.

Stephen Hawking's example proves that through perseverance, the extraordinary can become achievable. And despite his awful suffering, he now uses a surprising word to sum up his life. Because the progress of his disease has been slow enough for him to contribute so significantly to the world of science, he refers to himself as 'lucky'.

OPENING UP

➤ How do you believe you would cope if it was you in the wheelchair instead of Stephen Hawking? How do you think you would feel?

➤ Where do you think Stephen found the strength to pursue his ambitions?

➤ Do you believe Stephen really regards himself as 'lucky'? Why or why not?

DIGGING DEEPER

➤ How well do you cope when things go wrong? Do you persevere, or are you more likely to give up?

➤ Can you give an example of a situation where perseverance brought a reward? Can you think of a time when giving up has proved the wrong choice? Or perhaps the opposite has been true...

➤ Has suffering ever made you stronger? Explain your answer.

TAKING IT TO THE WORD

➤ **Read** James 1:2–12.

➤ How are these verses illustrated in the life of Stephen Hawking?

➤ How do you feel about the idea of feeling joy in trials and suffering?

➤ Why is perseverance a good and important thing?

➤ What do verses 9–10 mean? How can someone in humble circumstances also be in a high position?

➤ How might these verses encourage you to persevere? In what areas?

C22
THEME: **Atheism**

BIBLE: **Romans 1**

Atheism: the new cookery

Usually at Christmas time, the bestseller charts in bookshops and websites such as Amazon.com are dominated by 'gift' books: the latest collection of recipes from a celebrity chef, or amusing reflections on life from the year's most over-hyped comedian. In 2006, however, things seemed strangely out of order. The top-selling book of the season – rather ironically – was *The God Delusion*, an attempt by well-known atheist Richard Dawkins to argue that Christians, Muslims and other people of faith have got it all wrong.

According to Richard, there is no God. He argues that religion and faith are man-made ideas, manufactured thousands of years ago by people who realized that if they didn't believe in a God or gods, they'd all go mad. He believes so strongly not only that religion is wrong, but also that it can often be 'evil', he's devoted his life in recent years to doing all he can to prove the fact.

Among the scientific community, opinion about Richard is divided. Thanks to the success of his book, however, he's gained praise and support for his ideas from atheists all over the world. Armed with his arguments, many of them will now talk to their Christian friends and neighbours with renewed enthusiasm for their point of view.

However, for all Richard's success – including his handsome financial reward – the popularity of his book may actually undermine his case. After all, why are so many people rushing out to buy a book about God, if he's not worth bothering with? Perhaps the inbuilt thirst in every person to know the truth about God actually reveals the fact that someone placed it within them when they were created...

OPENING UP

➤ Why do you think Richard Dawkins is so desperate to disprove God's existence?

➤ How do you think God looks at Richard? Why?

➤ Do you think religion can sometimes be a bad thing? Explain your answer. Does this reflect more on God or on man?

DIGGING DEEPER

➤ Why might Richard's book actually be a good thing for the church? How could Christians engage positively with it?

➤ How do you react when someone challenges the things that you believe in most strongly?

➤ What do you think the average Christian's reaction to Richard and his book should be?

TAKING IT TO THE WORD

➤ **Read** Romans 1:16–23.

> ➤ Does creation prove God's existence? Why?

> ➤ Paul is quite matter-of-fact here – why does he say that atheists 'are without excuse'? What do you think that phrase means?

> ➤ How do verses 21–22 reflect on atheists like Richard?

> ➤ What are God's eternal power and divine nature? How do people of faith experience these 'invisible qualities' of God?

C23
THEME: **Death**
BIBLE: **Psalm 18**

'Fashionably late'

Kylie Minogue is one of the most popular and enduring female singers of the past few decades. She has legions of fans across the world, and has scored chart success repeatedly since way back in the 1980s. She is rich, beautiful, talented and much loved. In short, she is one of those girls who have everything.

In 2005, however, her perfect existence suddenly shifted into a nightmare. Midway through an international tour, Kylie was diagnosed with breast cancer – a disease which could be treated, but which had a very real chance of sending her to an early grave.

As she sought medical help in Australia, Kylie's popularity caused thousands of concerned fans to send messages of support, congregate outside her house and swamp her with get-well-soon cards. Faced with the thought of losing her, Kylie's home country collectively began to realize just how much they loved her. Their favourite daughter began chemotherapy treatment, and a nation held its breath.

Fortunately, there was good news around the corner. In 2006, Kylie's doctors announced that her cancer had been fought successfully, and the singer was now in remission. Within just a few months, Kylie announced that she was ready to perform again.

As she took the stage for her first live performance since her illness, she shared an emotional moment with the Sydney crowd. 'Sorry,' she joked after her year away, 'I was just being fashionably late.'

OPENING UP

➤ How did Kylie's brush with death show up the limits of her worldly success?

➤ How might you live differently if you had come close to dying?

➤ How do you think Kylie's experiences with cancer changed her attitudes?

DIGGING DEEPER

➤ Do you worry about dying young? Why or why not?

➤ Why might people fear death?

➤ What do you think happens to us when we die?

TAKING IT TO THE WORD

➤ **Read** Psalm 18:4–6.

➤ Does the psalmist's description of his fears about death sound familiar?

➤ What does this passage suggest about God and death?

➤ How easy or difficult do you find it to put your faith in God – that he will rescue you when you die?

C24
THEME: # The poor
BIBLE: # Acts 1

Changing a nation

Now one of the richest women in the world, TV host Oprah Winfrey started life in a very different situation. Born to a poor Baptist family in Mississippi, America, Oprah learnt from an early age that education was the only way to change her life.

With the support of her grandmother, Oprah skipped ahead two years at school and by age 13 had won a scholarship to study at a local high school, where she went on to become an honours student. She then studied Communication at university and became the first black female news anchor at a local Nashville TV channel.

As she became more successful in the media, Oprah donated money to many charities, including those helping the poor receive an education. But she wanted to offer more than just her money to those in need. After visiting South Africa's former President, Nelson Mandela, Oprah decided to build her own girls' school there.

Investing around £20 million, and interviewing many of the 3,500 applicants herself, Oprah was able to offer the gift of education to hundreds of poor girls. At the opening ceremony, she recalled her own impoverished childhood and said it was the proudest day of her life: 'When you educate a girl, you begin to change the face of a nation,' she declared.

OPENING UP

➤ Why do you think Oprah Winfrey places so much importance on the education of impoverished children?

➤ How do you think Oprah got to where she is today?

➤ What does her story make you think about your own life and ambitions?

DIGGING DEEPER

➤ Think about your own education. Do you ever consider yourself fortunate to have the chance to go to school? How else do you view school?

➤ What helps you to learn? Teachers? Interesting subjects? Self-discipline?

➤ Is education essential? List some people you consider to be successful who haven't received a full education. What does their success tell us?

TAKING IT TO THE WORD

➤ **Read** Acts 1:1–8.

➤ Jesus has spent three years teaching his disciples – yet he returns to 'teach about the kingdom' for another forty days. Why?

➤ Jesus turns his students loose to teach the world – what does this suggest to us about education?

➤ What do you know about Jesus' teaching style? How does it compare to school? What kind of school teacher do you think Jesus would have been?

➤ Why is it important for us to learn things before we're let loose on the world?

C25
THEME: **Names**
BIBLE: **John 1/Genesis 17**

What's in a name?

When celebrity couple Bob Geldof and Paula Yates had their second daughter, they decided to set her apart from other children by giving her an unusual name. They'd called their first daughter Fifi Trixibelle, but this time they wanted something even more striking. One can only imagine the expression on the vicar's face, then, when he christened Peaches Honeyblossom Michelle Charlotte Angel Vanessa Geldof.

Peaches is just one of a whole generation of celebrities' children with unconventional names. Musician Frank Zappa called his daughter Moon Unit, while David and Victoria Beckham famously named their boys Brooklyn, Romeo and Cruz. But Peaches, now 18, has sent shockwaves through the pages of celebrity magazines by declaring that she hates her name.

'I hate ridiculous names,' she said in one of the final issues of *Smash Hits*. 'My weird name has haunted me all my life.' Peaches hopes that her protest will discourage other celebrities from choosing bizarre baby names.

OPENING UP

➤ What do you think of such original celebrity baby names? Does Peaches' response make you feel differently, or more strongly about them?

➤ What do you think of your own name? Do you know what it means?

DIGGING DEEPER

➤ Look through some baby names and meanings. From the meanings, what kinds of names would you choose for yourself, or for your own children? Why?

➤ How important do you think a person's name is? Do you think it can define the way a person lives in any way?

➤ Have you ever thought of changing your name? Would you consider changing it? Why or why not? What effect might doing so have on your parents?

TAKING IT TO THE WORD

➤ **Read** John 1:40–42 and Genesis 17:1–6.

➤ Jesus changes Simon (which means 'reed') to Peter (which means 'rock'). God changes Abram ('exalted father') to Abraham ('father of a multitude'). Why do you think they made these changes? What does this tell us about names?

➤ Abram was old and unable to have children; Simon was going to deny Jesus three times. What do their new names tell us about the plans God had for them?

➤ Are unorthodox names like 'Peaches' giving more or less importance to the job of naming a child? Why?

Section D
The Bible in 25 Steps

Introduction

This final set of discussion starters is in some ways quite different to the previous three sets. It seeks to provide a journey through the main stories and themes of the Bible, from creation through to the promise of a new heaven and a new earth. It is not exhaustive, but in relatively few steps provides a gentle method for young people and groups to grasp a basic understanding of what happens in the Bible. This part of the book is therefore aimed mainly at Christian young people, and the guides in it will require more adapting for use with unchurched teenagers.

Each discussion starter unpacks a key event, character or theme, rooting it in a key Bible passage. There is no suggestion that these are the key twenty-five passages in the Bible, merely that these parts of the text are helpful in illustrating the key points and telling the over-arching story of the book. Fifteen of the discussions are based around Old Testament verses, with the other ten focusing on New Testament passages. The twenty-five guides are arranged in the order that the books appear in the Bible, rather than in chronological order (Job's appearance later in the Bible, for instance, probably does not accurately reflect his place in history).

Although I have attempted to steer away from areas of theological controversy where possible, difference on some issues is inevitable, and you may wish to rewrite some guides before using them with young people. And regardless of whether this proves an issue, the key to really making these guides work with a group is adaptation.

In this section, the discussion trigger and the three banks of questions serve slightly different purposes. Rather than just telling a story, the triggers themselves are designed as an introduction to both the story and the theme being covered. For this reason they are slightly longer than in previous sections.

The 'Opening up' questions relate mainly to the theme, while the 'Taking it to the Word' questions relate directly to the passage. Rather than providing a different direction in which to take the discussion, as before, the 'Digging deeper' questions are designed to complement the other two banks, and will either serve as a bridge between them, or help to flesh out one of those parts of the discussion.

When adapting these discussion triggers for use, then, you may wish to change the order in which these banks of questions appear – probably switching the second and third sets, and going directly to the text earlier in the meeting. In this series of discussions particularly, you may actually find it helpful to kick off your session by reading the passage, even before you read the trigger.

You may also wish to use these twenty-five guides in other ways. They may be suitable for personal reflection, if you provide young people with material for this; they may also work well in a cell-group context. Please be aware, however, as with the other guides, that by nature this book will provide and provoke more questions than it can possibly hope to answer! The idea of the discussion questions is to get young people thinking and talking about their world and their theology, but the responsibility may sometimes rest with the session leader to be able to provide a final answer to difficult questions – even if that answer is a genuine 'I'll get back to you!'

D1

THEME: # Creation (and evolution)
BIBLE: # Genesis 1

The Beginning

No one is totally sure when it happened, and few are arrogant enough to claim they know exactly how. One thing is sure though – at some point in time, the world we're standing on now came into being. There was a day when the earth burst into life.

The Bible describes it like this: God, the infinitely powerful being who has already created the entire universe, goes on to put the earth together – sculpting it out of apparently nothing. He starts, almost like an artist working with raw materials, with a 'formless and empty' earth, and then sets about his work, often simply speaking things into being. 'Let there be light,' he says, and there is. It seems to just appear on his word – he's *that* powerful!

His creation plan is ordered and meticulous, and the results are incredible. He divides land from sea, putting together oceans and continents. The vast array of trees, plants and vegetation that we take for granted is woven together by his hands. Animals, birds and fish follow. The entire animal kingdom comes about not by mistake, but by design. There's a plan to all this.

And last up, God pulls out his most incredible invention of all – us. He creates man and woman (and in some way they look like him), and he sets them up as rulers over everything that has been made before them. Then God sees all that he has made, and declares that it is 'very good'. The great artist stands back from the canvas, and is pleased with his work. As anyone who's ever seen a sunset or a mountain range or a laughing child will testify, he's quite right to be.

As the famous *Star Wars* tagline goes: 'Every story has a beginning... Every journey has a first step.' This is ours.

OPENING UP

➤ How do you believe we got here? Do you think the Bible's description of creation is accurate? Try to explain your answer.

➤ What do you find interesting about the way that God created the earth? How might he have done it differently?

➤ Why do you think God made man last?

DIGGING DEEPER

➤ Do you believe in evolution (the theory that the species naturally developed over millions of years)? Why?

➤ Do you think that there's a way that evolution and the Christian story of creation could in some way be compatible – could they *both* be right? Explain your answer.

➤ Scientists claim the world is millions of years old; some Christians think it's just a few thousand. What do you believe, and why?

TAKING IT TO THE WORD

➤ **Read** Genesis 1.

➤ We often think of God the Father as the force behind all this – but what do verses 2 and 26 suggest about the Trinity?

➤ Why do you think the Bible talks about six days? Could God really have made all this in 144 hours? Do you think he really did? Explain.

➤ What do you think God means when he gives his instruction to man in verses 28–30? What does this mean for us today?

D2
THEME: **Sin (and suffering)**
BIBLE: **Genesis 3**

Adam's fall

We've all made mistakes. We make them all the time. A little lie here; a mean word spoken there. It's part of human nature, isn't? The Bible says it is – but it also provides us with the story of how and why that capacity to do stuff wrong became part of humankind.

Adam and Eve are in the Garden of Eden, living with God, and life is pretty peachy. They're in charge of the earth – which is absolutely perfect, by the way – and they can do almost anything they like. They also get to live with God, and know him personally. They walk side by side with him, and since he's the guy who just created the universe, he's a pretty cool friend to have.

Of course, God says that they can do *almost* anything. There's one thing he says they can't do – eat the fruit of a single tree, or else they'll die. One tree. They're in paradise, in the middle of infinite beauty, and the only rule is that they can't eat the fruit of one tree. One tree out of probably thousands. Surely they can't mess that up...

A serpent appears (most scholars say this was the devil in the form of a creature), and unfortunately, the story goes downhill from there. He puts an idea into their heads, and incredibly, convinces them to rebel against God's one rule, and eat the fruit of the tree. God finds out and he's furious. He told them that if they ate the fruit of the tree they'd die, and now he has to see through his threat.

You can imagine God shaking his head in disbelief as his hand is forced and he has to take away the amazing privileges that he's given to Adam and Eve. They can no longer live forever; they can no longer live a life that's low on pain and high on pleasure. All because they ate from the tree, they're forced to leave paradise and enter the real world – taking evil with them.

Into God's perfect and marvellous creation, sin is brought. The world has not been the same since.

OPENING UP

➤ What do you think of this story? Do you believe this is something that really happened? Why or why not?

➤ Put yourself in the shoes of Adam and Eve – what do you think you would have done when the serpent spoke?

➤ What do you think of God's reaction? Do you think he is fair or unfair to them?

DIGGING DEEPER

➤ What do you think the consequences of this story (often called 'the fall of man') have been throughout history?

➤ What do you think were the consequences for God's creation? You might find Romans 8:18–22 interesting here.

➤ Why do you think God allows good people to suffer? Explain your answer.

TAKING IT TO THE WORD

➤ **Read** Genesis 3.

➤ Adam blames Eve – what do you think about that? Is he right? Is this verse (verse 12) relevant today?

➤ After he has become angry, God makes clothes for Adam and Eve. What does this tell us about his character?

➤ We know that this isn't the end of the story. What does this passage suggest about the future paradise that Christians can look forward to?

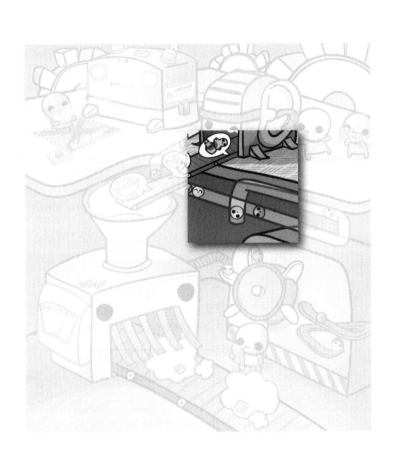

D3

THEME: **God's people**

BIBLE: **Genesis 15**

Abram's call

It would be so much easier if God did everything himself. But he didn't make that choice, and he doesn't today. God uses people – flawed humans like you and me – to carry out his plan here on earth.

The people God chose to use – 'God's people', as they have become known – started with a most unlikely source. Abram was an old man – 100 years old, in fact, and he and his wife Sarai had no children. Yet God promised him that his people would somehow spring from Abram's line. At his age, he had difficulty believing God's promise that he would become a father. It's a protest that we can all understand – after all, you don't see many 100-year-olds standing there looking proud in your local maternity unit.

God insists, though, that his descendants will be as great in number as the stars in the sky. At which point, however crazy it sounds, Abram believes him. God is pleased, and reveals more of his plan to his wide-eyed old listener. Abram falls into a deep sleep, and God explains that his descendants will suffer great trials, but that ultimately they will be rescued. Well ahead of time, God correctly predicts everything that is going to happen in the first part of the Old Testament. It starts just a little later, with the birth of Abram's first son.

God's people do suffer slavery, persecution and trials – but ultimately the line isn't broken, and eventually Jesus appears as part of the family. Joseph – Jesus' 'earth dad' – is descended directly from Abram, whom God later renames 'Abraham'. From this 100-year-old expectant father, the whole of Jewish history springs – from pain through to redemption. God has chosen his people, and he chooses the most unlikely man to start it all off.

OPENING UP

➤ Do you believe this story really happened? Do you think a child was born to a 100-year-old couple?

➤ Why do you think this story is important to Jewish history? And to us today?

➤ How do you think it would have felt for Abram to hear that his children and descendants were headed for pain, suffering and slavery?

DIGGING DEEPER

➤ Why do you think God chooses to use people to accomplish his plans and purposes? Why not just do everything himself?

➤ Do you feel like part of God's people? Why or why not?

➤ Do you think it's important or significant that Christians today are part of a story and a people that stretches back thousands of years? Explain your answer.

TAKING IT TO THE WORD

➤ **Read** Genesis 15.

➤ How do you think Abram and Sarai would have felt about their future before this? How might it have felt to hear that they were about to start a family?

➤ Why do you think Abram felt 'a thick and dreadful darkness' in his dream (verse 12)?

➤ What do you think it meant for God to make a 'covenant' with Abram? What were the results?

➤ Why do you think God was going to put Abram's descendants through so much pain?

➤ What does it mean to you to be part of God's people?

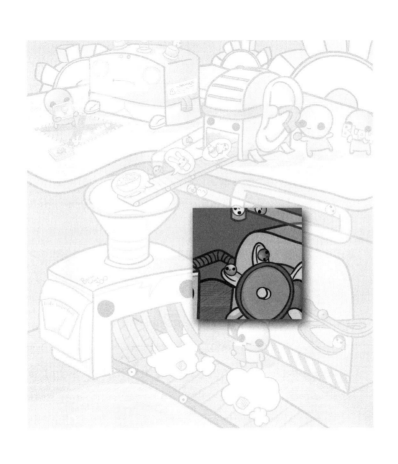

D4
THEME: # God hears the cry
BIBLE: # Exodus 3

The rescue

Just as God has predicted to Abram, the Israelites –
God's people – find themselves in slavery in Egypt,
North Africa. As slaves they have no rights, no pleasures, no possessions. Their lives involve making bricks,
all day long, seven days a week. Anyone who questions
how Egyptian buildings such as the pyramids were built
will realize that they would have needed a huge work-
force. They did – and it was the forced labour of God's
people that helped to create the splendour of the
Egyptian skyline.

Working flat out, all day, all week, all year, was no
life. God's people were reduced to a state below what
we would consider humanity. If they didn't work, they
were executed like dogs. When we imagine the
Israelites in slavery, we need to put aside the childish
notions put across in school assemblies or Bible story
cartoons. Being a slave in Egypt was a living hell.

So what do the people of God do? They cry out.
Together and alone, they cry out from the pit of despair
to the God they have deserted, and ask him to step in –

to save them. They sing, they pray, they cry: 'God, save us.'

What does God do? He hears the cry. Not only does he hear it, he constructs his escape plan, and moves in. He chooses a shepherd, Moses, as the man who is going to lead his people out of slavery in Egypt, and he reveals his plan in the most spectacular circumstances. An angel leads Moses to a bush that seems to be on fire, but somehow isn't actually burning, and from within the bush, the voice of God speaks.

God tells Moses that he has both 'heard the cry' of his people, and is 'concerned about their suffering'. He's going to use Moses to get them out. He's going to strike the Egyptians with everything he's got, and Moses is going to be his mouthpiece. Despite Moses' nervousness, God is insistent.

The rescue is on.

OPENING UP

➤ What do you think it must have been like to be a slave in Egypt? What do you think you would do if you lived in conditions like those described?

➤ What do you think would happen to you if had to work all day, every day, every week?

➤ How bad do things have to get for people to cry out to God? What makes you cry out to God?

DIGGING DEEPER

➤ What would you do if you knew that people lived under the same circumstances as the Israelites in Egypt, today? Are there people who live like that?

➤ What is slavery? How are people enslaved today?

➤ How can we help people, and ourselves, to escape from these kinds of slavery?

TAKING IT TO THE WORD

➤ **Read** Exodus 3.

➤ Do you think it's significant that God uses a shepherd for this job (verse 1)?

➤ What does God mean when he tells Moses he stands on 'holy ground' (verse 5)? Was it always holy? Is it just that piece of ground? Why?

➤ What do these verses (particularly 7–10) tell us about the character of God? How is this important to us today?

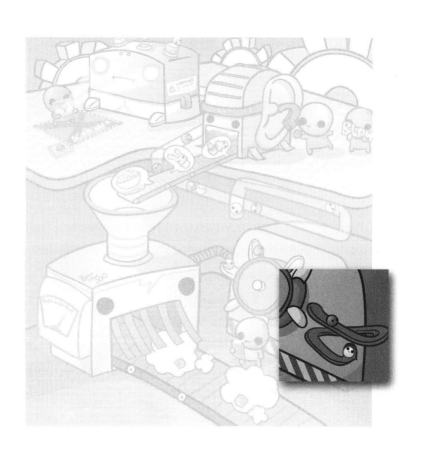

D5

THEME: **The law (and rules)**

BIBLE: **Leviticus 14**

Rules for a reason

The Old Testament is full of some pretty strange rules and regulations. From snigger-worthy material about bodily functions through to a whole section on mildew, the law that God gave to Moses covers some pretty weird territory. Or at least, that's how it seems to us now.

Back then, when the law was given to a real group of people at a real time, it made a whole lot of sense. God's people had just come out of a life of slavery in Egypt. And it wasn't nice, friendly, picture-book slavery – it was a sub-human existence, where every day involved long, boring, painful hours of work, and nothing else. This lasted for 400 years, before God heard the cry of his people and brought them out into freedom. Problem was, after four centuries in this hideous existence, God's people had forgotten how to live in freedom. They'd forgotten how to be human.

For them, then, the law wasn't a weird collection of rules and things to hold them back – it was exactly what they needed. Without rules that told them how to deal with infectious skin diseases, for instance, they soon would have had epidemics on their hands. They needed the law to tell them how to avoid that kind of disaster.

That's not all the law was for, of course. God's people kept messing up, making mistakes, big and small, that separated them from him. In order that he might remain close to them, God introduced through the law a system of animal sacrifices, to act as a kind of physical apology to God. It wasn't just about needlessly slaughtering animals – in those days of few possessions, it must have hurt an Israelite to give up a prize animal to make up for something that they had done wrong. But of course, that was exactly the point – that was what made it a sacrifice.

Skip forward to Jesus, hanging there on the cross, and we see a very similar situation unfolding. Mankind has done things wrong – millions and billions of things wrong. There aren't enough animals alive to make up for all the wrongs they've committed. In Jesus, however, God has provided one once-and-for-all super-sacrifice. Through his death, man and God can again be together.

OPENING UP

➤ What are the rules that govern your life? Where do they come from?

➤ Are there some rules that you dislike, or sometimes break? Explain.

➤ Do you see Christianity as a faith full of rules? Why?

DIGGING DEEPER

➤ If you were your country's leader, what law would you introduce, and why?

➤ What current rule or law might you remove, and why?

➤ What do you think the consequences should be for people who repeatedly break laws? What should they have to do to make up for it?

TAKING IT TO THE WORD

➤ **Read** Leviticus 14:1–32.

➤ Where do you see the different elements of the law at work in this passage? Which parts are common sense, and which parts deal with sin?

➤ Why do you think it was so important that these instructions were given to God's people then?

➤ Do you think these verses still have something to say to us today? Explain your answer.

➤ How does Jesus' sacrifice on the cross relate to the law?

D6

THEME: # God's supreme power

BIBLE: # Joshua 6

Out of Jericho's ruins

Have you ever been in a situation that seemed completely impossible? Faced the kind of problem that only a miracle could fix? That's how it was for Joshua.

His enemies lived in Jericho – an incredible city with massive walls that no army could penetrate. There was no human way that, as leader of the Israelite army, Joshua could expect to take Jericho in battle. The odds were stacked so firmly against him, that a modern equivalent might be a local store trying to beat the profits of the big shopping mall. It was a real David vs. Goliath affair – but then again, God seems to like those kinds of odds.

Encouraged by God's promise that somehow the battle would be won, Joshua takes his army down to Jericho, and follows the instructions carefully. He is told to march around the edge of the city with the entire army, for six days. When the seventh day comes, God tells him to march around seven further times, blow the trumpets and shout. From a military point of view, it sounds like a rubbish plan, frankly. Yet God tells him to do it, and he does.

On the seventh day, the trumpets sound, and the Israelites give their shout – hoping that God will come through and deliver the great city into their hands. And of course, he does. The gigantic walls literally collapse in front of their eyes, and the Israelite army surge in and take their enemies by surprise.

Joshua's impossible situation is made possible by the hand of God.

OPENING UP

➤ This is a very strange story. Do you think it really happened? Why or why not?

➤ Why do you think God chose to defeat Jericho in this way?

➤ What does this story suggest about God's power? Do you imagine that God still has this much power today? Explain your answer.

DIGGING DEEPER

➤ What is your personal Jericho? What is the impossible thing that you, or a friend or family member, need a miracle to achieve right now?

➤ How do you think the average person would advise you to approach that situation?

➤ What do you think God's response would be?

➤ It's amazing how even Christians can carry their problems around without ever bringing them to God. If appropriate, take a moment to ask God for his help with the 'Jericho problem' you've just identified.

TAKING IT TO THE WORD

➤ **Read** Joshua 6.

> ➤ What do you think about the way God deals with his enemies here? Do you think it's fair? Explain your answer.

> ➤ What do we learn about God from this passage? What do we learn about Joshua from the way he is prepared to carry out God's bizarre plan? Is there a lesson for us here?

> ➤ What do you think verses 18–19 are all about? Is God greedy? Or is something else going on?

> ➤ How obedient do you think you would be if God asked you to do something? What if he asked you to give £50 to the poor? What about if he asked you to leave your family and friends and move to Africa to work with those same poor people?

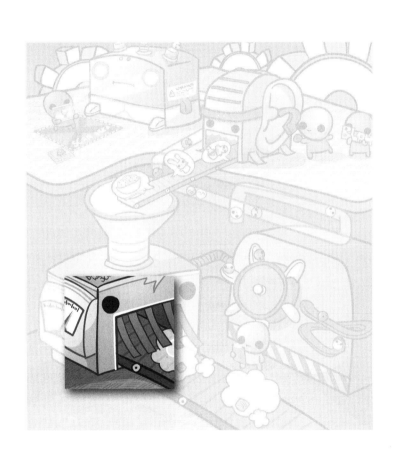

D7
THEME: **Israel's greatest king**
BIBLE: **2 Samuel 9**

David's heart

We all know people who are less fortunate than us. The choice we have is pretty simple – either we decide to ignore them and focus on our own lives, however perfect or problematic they might be; or else we roll our sleeves up, and pitch in to help. Modern life is hectic, and we've developed quick-fix ways of helping (which are of genuine benefit) such as giving money to charities who can roll their sleeves up and get their hands dirty instead.

As a great and much-loved king, David could easily have been forgiven for taking this kind of approach. From his high office, it would have been natural for him to appoint some do-gooders to work among the poor on his behalf.

That's not what he chose to do, however. One of the stories about David's life that appears in the Bible concerns his visit to Mephibosheth, a lowly grandson of David's predecessor King Saul, and a social outcast because he was crippled in both feet (in a day when people believed the crippled were being punished by God). Considering that he was a king, the love and kindness that David shows to this man would have been astonishing to those around him. He ensures that Mephibosheth and his family are looked after, and even insists that he takes a place at David's own table at Jerusalem. It's a safe assumption that there wouldn't have been too many disabled people around that table...

Through his actions, we see another side to David, often seen as a great leader, general and warrior. More importantly, we see evidence of God's influence on him. David lived his life in a close relationship with God, and as a result, he became infected by God's heart for the poor and the oppressed.

OPENING UP

➤ What's your attitude to people in need? What do you feel when you hear about suffering, poverty and injustice in different parts of the world?

➤ What does David's response to Mephibosheth tell us about him? Do you think this side of his nature made him a stronger or a weaker king? What about in the eyes of others?

➤ List some great leaders from history. What do you think their attitude to the poor and oppressed was?

DIGGING DEEPER

➤ Mephibosheth says he sees himself like 'a dead dog'. Why do you think he feels like that?

➤ Do you know people who feel that way about themselves? How do you relate to them? Could you help them more?

➤ Identify opportunities to help individuals who are in need – not just at a distance, but up close, like David did.

TAKING IT TO THE WORD

➤ **Read** 2 Samuel 9.

➤ David's friendship with Jonathan (see 1 Samuel 20) inspires him to show kindness. How do your friendships inspire others? Do they? How could you live differently in order to create this effect?

➤ David doesn't just wait for needy people to knock on his door – he seeks out the opportunity to do good. What does this tell us about him? Do you look for these opportunities?

➤ What do you think it meant for Mephibosheth to eat at the king's table? What would it have done for Mephibosheth? What message would it have given to onlookers?

D8

THEME: God speaks through his prophets

BIBLE: 1 Kings 18

Elijah on Mount Carmel

Even though their recent history had been littered with examples of God demonstrating his power, the Israelites continued to rebel against him, over and again. If Israel had one good king who led the people in the ways of God, it was a pretty safe bet that the next one would be a stinker, setting up altars to false gods and generally doing evil. To confuse matters, after the death of David's son Solomon, the kingdom of the Israelites was divided into two parts, Israel and Judah. As a rule, Judah had some fairly good kings, whereas the larger kingdom of Israel seemed to produce more rotten apples.

Ahab was such a king – a man who had become a follower of the god Baal, despite being the leader of Israel. Ahab's actions angered God (pretty understandably – God had prospered Israel for many years; now they were turning their backs on him for the sake of a man-made idol), and so he sent his top man on earth at the time, the prophet Elijah, to sort things out.

Like God, Elijah is fed up with the worship of this

false god, and so sets up a competition between his God and Baal. He challenges Ahab to send all the prophets of false gods in Israel (a whopping 950 of them) to join him on Mount Carmel. Elijah will build an altar of wood, and put a sacrificial bull on it, and the 950 prophets are to build another. The competition is this: both teams are to call on the name of their God or god, and the one who sends down fire to consume the sacrifice is the real God.

The 950 are pretty confident – after all, there's strength in numbers, isn't there? Standing there alone, however, Elijah knows he's about to be handing out the 'I told you so's'. The prophets of Baal do their best to get a response from the heavens, but after a whole day of frantic prayer, nothing happens. You can imagine Elijah's fairly self-confident expression as he stands up to respond, and the fire of God entirely consumes both the sacrifice and the altar.

As they're led off to be executed, the prophets of Baal probably begin to wish they'd listened to Elijah earlier...

OPENING UP

➤ Do you think this passage suggests that it's OK to put God to the test? Explain your answer.

➤ How do you think you would have felt, as a prophet of Baal, when God destroyed the offering?

➤ What kinds of false gods or idols do people follow today? How do you think God feels about that?

DIGGING DEEPER

➤ Why do you think God speaks through people (prophets)?

➤ Do you believe there are still prophets today? Do you know any?

➤ Do you believe that it's possible for you to prophesy – for God to speak through you to others? Explain your answer, and take a look at 1 Corinthians 14 if you want to explore this question further.

TAKING IT TO THE WORD

➤ **Read** 1 Kings 18:16–46.

➤ How do you think it was possible that God's people – having lived in a time of such signs and wonders – could begin to worship other gods?

➤ Why do you think Elijah goes the extra mile and has water poured onto the offering? What does this tell us about him?

➤ What does verse 21 suggest about people's unwillingness to commit? Consider if this verse applies particularly to you at the moment (you're probably not following Baal, but you get the idea).

➤ In verse 46, God gives Elijah super powers! How does this fit in with your idea of what God can do when he uses people?

D9

THEME: **Power**

BIBLE: **2 Chronicles 9**

Solomon's corruption

There are some stories in the Bible that require a second reading. It might appear on the surface that one thing is going on, when really there's something far bigger bubbling under the surface. That's arguably what's going on in the story of Solomon in 2 Chronicles, which focuses triumphantly on the greatness of this king, the son of David who was widely regarded as the wisest man who ever lived.

Clearly, Solomon's wisdom was beyond dispute. He wrote most of the Book of Proverbs, which has become a moral backbone for much of civilization, and he performed great feats of judgment over his people. Yet for all his great contemplation and wisdom, he had a weakness. Material wealth, and awesome power over the kingdom, corrupted him.

There's a saying that 'power corrupts, and absolute power corrupts absolutely', and it's often been proven true. There are many famous stories of men who sacrificed their morals to obtain riches, or people in power who've done *whatever* was needed to ensure they didn't lose their position. In other cases, the corruption is much more subtle, and that's how it was with Solomon.

Solomon believed that he was following God's heart, just as his father had done. When we analyse his actions, however, something doesn't add up. When the great Queen of Sheba pays this fellow Royal a visit, she is struck and impressed (in fact, 'overwhelmed') by many things: 'the food on his table, the seating of his officials, the attending servants in their robes, the cup-bearers in their robes...' (verse 4). These are certainly impressive – but do they really fit in with what we know about God's way?

Because if all this wealth is being stored in Solomon's courts – what's going on outside them? In fact, in order to realize his ambition of building the ulti-mate temple and palace, he decrees that foreigners liv-ing among the Israelites should be rounded up and forced into labour. In other words, he reintroduces slav-ery. And since he forces the foreigners into labour, rather than his own people, you could say that... he becomes Pharaoh.

So while 2 Chronicles appears to focus a spotlight on the greatness of Solomon, it is actually illuminating his weaknesses. Far from being a great and Godly leader, he is actually responsible for helping one of the worst parts of his people's history to repeat itself.

OPENING UP

➤ From what you may already know, and from this story, what kind of leader do you think Solomon was?

➤ If Solomon was so wise, why do you think he amassed so much wealth and power?

➤ What do you make of Solomon's decision to employ slaves? Why do you think he chose only to force foreigners into labour?

DIGGING DEEPER

➤ Who are the people who have power over you? Explain your answers.

➤ Who do you think are the most powerful people in this country, and in the world?

➤ How do they use their power? Who do you believe uses their power well... and not so well?

TAKING IT TO THE WORD

➤ **Read** 2 Chronicles 9:1–13.

➤ How do you think the writer of this passage wants us to view Solomon?

➤ What do you think about the number of talents that Solomon receives? Coincidence...?

➤ Why do you think the queen wanted to test Solomon with hard questions?

➤ How do you feel Solomon has used his power? What kind of leader do you think he was?

D10
THEME: # Faith in suffering
BIBLE: # Job 1

Good Job

How do you cope when things go wrong? How well do you think you'd do if absolutely everything you knew and loved came crashing apart around you?

Probably not as well as Job, the man who is famous for having possibly the worst day in history. He was a great man, and a Godly man, with a nice house, a large family and plenty of camels. He was referred to as 'the greatest man among all the people of the East'.

One day, right in the middle of enjoying his until-then marvellous life, Job hears some bad news. A servant tells him that all his oxen and donkeys have been stolen, and his other servants murdered. Moments later, two other messengers appear, to reveal that the same has happened to his sheep, his camels and the servants who worked with them. And before Job even has a chance to take it all in, a fourth man arrives with the most terrible news of all – the house of Job's son has collapsed suddenly, killing every one of Job's children. It's a miracle that Job isn't killed by the shock of it all.

According to the Bible, Job's suffering is the work of

Satan himself. God is so convinced of Job's great character, that he allows the devil to wreak havoc on his life. God believes in Job – and knows that even in the face of great adversity, he'll maintain his faith.

God's trust is well placed – incredibly, Job's response to the news is to fall to the ground and worship. He is even able, in this moment of great tragedy, to be philosophical, speaking the immortal words: 'The Lord gave and the Lord has taken away; may the name of the Lord be praised.'

Could any of us really say we'd react in the same way?

OPENING UP

➤ Do you believe this really happened to a real person, and that he reacted in this way? Why or why not?

➤ What do you think of Job's reaction?

➤ How do you feel about the fact that God allows Job to go through all this?

➤ Do you think Job's happy existence up to this point made all this pain easier or harder to bear? Explain your answer.

DIGGING DEEPER

➤ Why do you think God allows suffering? What would you say to someone who asked you this question – particularly if they've suffered badly themselves?

➤ Do you think all suffering is the result of this kind of testing? Why or why not?

➤ What else might cause suffering? (Romans 8:18–22 may help to explain why natural disasters occur.)

➤ What role do people have in each other's suffering?

TAKING IT TO THE WORD

➤ **Read** Job 1.

➤ What do we learn about Job before things go wrong?

➤ What do we learn about Satan in verse 7?

➤ Why do you think God allowed Satan to test Job?

➤ What do you think we can learn from what we see of Job's character after things go wrong?

D11
THEME: **Worship**
BIBLE: **Psalm 23**

David's Psalms

David was a very impressive man. Not only was he the mighty warrior who defeated great armies and won every battle, not to mention a great leader who commanded respect; he was also a fine poet and musician. His lyrics, scattered throughout the Book of Psalms, are among the most-published song-words in history!

Inspired by a desire to be close to and worship his God, David took time out of his frantic life to compose many songs, and in his role as 'Israel's singer of songs' (see 2 Samuel 23:1) he also performed them. Not just a leader of armies, then – David was also the big-name worship leader of his day.

David's talent for songwriting is one way in which God's character has in effect 'rubbed off' on him. Through having a close relationship with God, David learns and naturally takes on some of his Creator's characteristics (such as his concern for the oppressed, as seen in his care for Mephibosheth), and creativity is a key part of God's make-up. Through knowing God so well, his heart's response is also simply to worship him with great thanksgiving. Out of a combination of these two factors, David's Psalms spring.

In Psalm 23, David is in reflective mood. In these simple, very famous words, he gratefully outlines the nature of his relationship with God – who looks after him and cares for him. As a king who was once a shepherd himself, David is humble enough to be shepherded by the true king over all.

OPENING UP

➤ What do you think is the purpose of worship? Why do Christians do it?

➤ What have been your experiences of Christian worship? What goes through your head when you are singing or experiencing it?

➤ Is worship just about music, or something else? If so, what?

DIGGING DEEPER

➤ Do you think of yourself as a 'creative' person? Why or why not?

➤ Creativity is a key part of God's make-up – and we are made in his image. Does this mean creativity is something that everyone has, hidden away somewhere, or even something that they can learn?

➤ How do you express yourself creatively? How might you use that creativity to worship God (think beyond music)?

TAKING IT TO THE WORD

➤ **Read** Psalm 23.

     ➤ Moses was a shepherd. David was a shepherd – do you think this word might be more significant than we sometimes think? What does it mean?

     ➤ Why do you think David says he walks through the valley of the shadow of death'? What does that phrase mean to you?

     ➤ What do we learn about David from this Psalm?

     ➤ What do we learn about God?

     ➤ Consider writing your own short Psalm or song to God, as a response to this passage. How do you feel about God's presence in your life?

D12
THEME: **Wisdom (and guidance)**
BIBLE: **Proverbs 3**

Wise words

We could all do with being a bit wiser. Whether it's our words, our decisions or our actions, we've all been guilty of errors of judgment, and sometimes they can be very costly.

Celebrity-obsessed tabloid magazines love this kind of stuff. They can't wait to tell us which movie star has picked out the wrong dress for the award ceremony, or which politician has got his secretary pregnant. It's what sells magazines, of course – because we love to laugh at people who've been even stupider than us!

Right in the middle of the Bible, the Book of Proverbs can be found, containing a collection of wise words from people whom God had gifted with extreme wisdom. They aren't laws like those found in the books of Moses, but they are practical words of guidance, written by Godly people who were probably wiser than us.

The opening chapters of Proverbs explain the bene-fits of wisdom, and particularly the wisdom of following the ways of God. To 'trust in the Lord with all your heart and lean not on your own understanding' is at the heart of the thinking here. If the reader follows the wisdom of God, he or she is encouraged with the promise of long life, prosperity, favour and 'a good name in the sight of God and man'. All of these things are desirable, and hard to reach. Perhaps that's why the Book of Proverbs is popular with people who perhaps don't share the Christian or Jewish faiths, but are looking hard for answers.

Christians know there's more to these words than simple human wisdom. They are divinely inspired, and since true wisdom comes only from God, they are a good reference for those seeking to become more like him.

OPENING UP

➤ What does it mean to be wise? Do you desire wisdom? Why or why not? If so, how high is it on your wish list?

➤ Who do you know who you believe to be wise? What makes them wise?

➤ What are some of the things that people have done recently, that have made the news and could be considered 'unwise'?

DIGGING DEEPER

➤ Where do you look for guidance when you have big decisions to make or problems to face? Do you think you're looking in the best places for this advice?

➤ Do you believe that God guides us? How has he guided you?

➤ How could someone find a good balance between the advice of people and the Word of God, when looking for guidance?

TAKING IT TO THE WORD

➤ **Read** Proverbs 3.

➤ Why do you think the writer suggests that following the Proverbs could make your life longer, make you richer, and more (verses 1–4)?

➤ What does it mean to 'not be wise in your own eyes' (verse 7)?

➤ Why might honouring the Lord with wealth lead to your barns overflowing (or a modern equivalent!)?

➤ Which of these proverbs do you find most interesting or helpful?

➤ Try to pick one piece of guidance from this passage that you will attempt to follow this week. Write it down somewhere where you are likely to return to it over and again. Pray that God will help you to be wise, and to follow his guidance.

D13
THEME: A coming Messiah (hope)
BIBLE: Isaiah 8 – 9

A new hope

Seven hundred years before Jesus was born, God let his people know that he was on his way. His coming was predicted by God's prophets – men who had devoted their lives to bringing messages from God to the people. Often they would bring warnings, or try to persuade the people to return to their God, but they also brought a message of hope – that in the future, God was going to make something spectacular happen, and remove the boundary between man and God forever.

The author of one of the Bible's longest books, Isaiah is reckoned to have spent more than sixty years as a prophet to the people of Israel. In that time he brought many words to the people, but perhaps the most exciting of all can be found eight chapters into his book.

The people of God have again abandoned him, and are looking for answers in all the wrong places. They've believed the lie that God is nowhere to be found, and are consulting mediums and 'spiritists' instead. Isaiah warns the people not to be so foolish – a 'great light' from God is around the corner. A child is about to be born – 'and the government will be on his shoulders'. Isaiah knew what this meant – as did his listeners. A Messiah, one who was given the power of God, was on the way.

Over the next few hundred years, the Jewish people would wait patiently for a Messiah. They expected a mighty warrior who would liberate them from all oppression and install them as rulers over the earth. To those people, Jesus must have come as quite a shock.

OPENING UP

➤ Did you know that Jesus appeared in the Old Testament? Do you know of other places in the Old Testament where he appears? What does this tell you about the relationship between the Old and New Testaments?

➤ Why do you think God told his people about Jesus in advance?

➤ How do you think it would have felt to hear these words from the mouth of a prophet who was totally trusted and had a history of getting things like this right?

DIGGING DEEPER

➤ What is hope?

➤ What do you hope for? In the future? This week?

➤ What do you hope will happen to the community around you? How can you help to make that hope into a reality?

TAKING IT TO THE WORD

➤ **Read** Isaiah 8:16 – 9:7.

> ➤ Does 8:21 feel relevant today? Are there people who act and feel in this way?

> ➤ What kind of Saviour might you expect to come, from reading these words?

> ➤ What clues do we find in these verses that point to the Jesus who really came?

> ➤ What does 9:7 mean to you? When do you believe this part of the prophecy did or will come true?

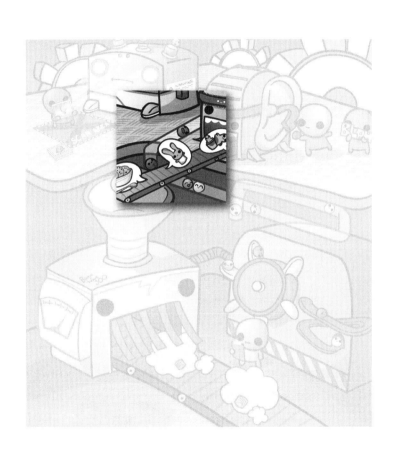

D14
THEME: Renewal (and life balance)
BIBLE: Ezekiel 37

Dry bones

People have a tendency to make a mess of things, to take a wrong turn, and eventually burn out. We live too much of our lives at or above the speed limit, and it's often the most important things and people that suffer as a result. Whether it's spending too long on the Xbox and not enough time studying, or the other way around, as a race we don't seem to be all that good at achieving balance, and all too often we end up tired or exhausted.

Spiritually, it can be the same story. At times we can feel close to God; often we can feel empty and far from him. Fortunately, God loves to renew his people, both physically and spiritually; both individually and together. Today, he provides his Spirit to live within us and keep the engine running smoothly. In the days of the Old Testament, he constantly heard the cry of his people, and responded to them.

We may not quite identify with the following picture provided by the prophet Ezekiel, but his first listeners certainly would have done. God led Ezekiel into a valley, on the floor of which he saw many dry bones. As he prophesied over them, God showed him a vision – the dry bones rose up, took on tendons, skin and even breath. Then, as he looked at the vast army of men now standing before him, Ezekiel heard again from God, who explained that these bones represented the entire nation of Israel, and that he was going to bring renewal among them.

God's people had been on a long journey. Into slavery, out and back again. These words would have been both a damning verdict on their spiritual deadness, and an extraordinary encouragement that God was still among them, and still had a great plan for their future. In Jesus, it would one day be revealed.

OPENING UP

➤ What do you understand by the word 'renewal'? What does it mean to renew something? Think about the way the word is made up: 're' and 'new'.

➤ What people, buildings, areas or brands can you think of that have been renewed? What has this done for them?

➤ What would it look like for you to be 'renewed' personally, physically, and spiritually?

DIGGING DEEPER

➤ What does the picture of a valley of dry bones say to you, and to your life? Do you identify with it?

➤ How good are you at maintaining a good balance between working and playing? Where does God fit in?

➤ Are you good at resting? What do you do to properly rest, and how often does it happen?

TAKING IT TO THE WORD

➤ **Read** Ezekiel 37:1–14.

➤ How do you think it would have felt, as an Israelite, to hear this prophecy first hand? Would you be inspired or offended? Explain your answer.

➤ Do you think the original listeners would have wanted renewal? Do you today?

➤ What else strikes you as interesting in this strange story? What do you think it has to say to us today?

➤ How is this prophecy fulfilled by Jesus' resurrection, and the coming of the Holy Spirit (see Acts 2)?

D15
THEME: **Punishment and restoration**

BIBLE: **Hosea 1**

An unfaithful wife

The Book of Hosea contains an interesting twist. Rather than just have the prophet Hosea join with his contemporaries in urging Israel to change its ways, God asks Hosea to use his life to provide a visual aid for the people, who just aren't getting it. In a way, you could say that God is appealing to different learning styles...

He asks Hosea to find himself 'an adulterous wife and children of unfaithfulness'. It's probably not the most thrilling proposition for a man, but Hosea loves God, and obeys him. He marries Gomer, who sleeps with other men and is also a prostitute. 'Good choice, Hosea,' his dinner-party friends might not have commented.

Hosea gives his children names that are of prophetic significance to Israel, and then steps away from his unfaithful wife. However, after a period of separation he has compassion and takes her back. He insists that she gives up her unfaithfulness, and they are reconciled.

This vivid picture provides the beating heart of

Hosea's message – and provides a striking metaphor for what had been happening in the relationship between God and Israel. God's people have been unfaithful to him, over and over again. In a sense, they have prostituted themselves to other gods.

Yet despite his anger, and his promise to punish Israel, he already has one eye on restoration. He just loves his people too much to turn his back on them. So, just as Hosea is reconciled to Gomer, God promises that he'll take his people back too.

OPENING UP

➤ How do you think it would have felt for Hosea to knowingly take on a wife who was guaranteed to break his heart?

➤ What do you think the people around Hosea would have advised him?

➤ How do you feel about the fact that God asked him to do it? Why do you think he did ask him?

➤ Do you think it would have been possible for Hosea to truly love Gomer in the end? Why or why not?

DIGGING DEEPER

➤ What are some of the parallels between Hosea's story and God's story?

➤ How might another man have treated Gomer differently? How else might God have dealt with Israel?

➤ What do we learn about God from his persistent pursuit of Israel, even though his people keep breaking his heart?

TAKING IT TO THE WORD

➤ **Read** Hosea 1.

> ➤ Do you find these verses hard? Why are they difficult to read?
>
> ➤ Even as early as verse 10 of chapter 1, God is already talking positively, and hinting that there'll be a happy ending. How does this change the nature of the passage?
>
> ➤ Verses 4 and 11 seem almost to contradict each other. What's going on here?
>
> ➤ What is your relationship with God like? Are you following him closely, or distracted by other 'gods' and idols? If appropriate, pray together that your focus will be right, and honouring to him.

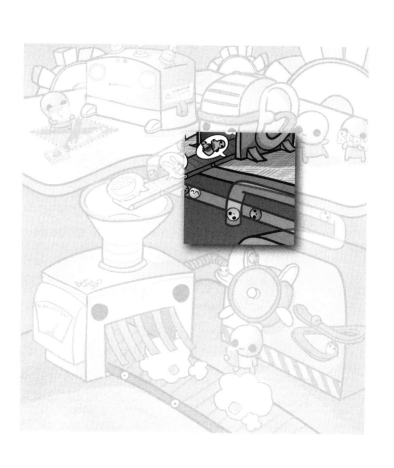

D16
THEME: # God sends his Son
BIBLE: # Luke 2

God is breast-feeding

There are some stories that we've heard so many times, that it's hard to really hear them any more. Jesus' birth is a bit like this. For many of us, we've seen (and acted in) so many school nativities, and watched so many cheesy TV Christmas shows, that we've become completely numbed to the story. Which is a shame, considering it's one of the three most significant events in human history.

But if you've ever thought that the nativity story was, well, a little uninspiring, you're not alone. It was what the religious people thought at the time. Their prophets had been telling them God was going to send a Saviour. And since they were oppressed by the Roman empire and had lost their freedom, to them a Saviour was going to look a lot more like Arnold Schwarzenegger.

So when a little baby arrived – not born into some great royal family, but into total squalor – they were probably a little confused. And when he grew up, preaching love, humility and turning the other cheek, they became convinced that this was the wrong man.

This guy just couldn't have been the Saviour who the prophets had been predicting.

But he was. The miracles he performed, and the fact that he rose from the dead, convinced enough people to start a movement, which today has around two billion professing believers. The words he spoke were so wise, so unearthly, that he's now regarded as one of the greatest teachers of all time – whoever you believe he was.

Here's what happened: God, seeing that Paradise hadn't been enough, realizing that choosing a people and teaching them how to live hadn't been enough, takes the most drastic action. He sends his own Son – who is fully God – to earth. That moment is pivotal in human history – because God comes to earth to open up the way back to him. Through his Son, God and humankind will again be able to look one another in the eye.

And so Jesus – this eternal, all-powerful being – is incarnated as a human. He can feel pain, physical weakness, tiredness. But even more than that, God doesn't just make Jesus appear, all grown up and full of great wisdom. He brings him into the world through childbirth – as a tiny, frail, helpless baby.

So here we are, back at that famous nativity scene. And to me, it doesn't seem uninspiring at all: the shepherds and the wise men, crowding round his manger, because they're in on the secret that God has just moved into the neighbourhood; the little donkey who prevented the baby from being born in the desert somewhere by bringing his mother to this place of relative safety; and Mary, with the baby Jesus, feeding at her breast.

God is breast-feeding. Perhaps that's the most remarkable picture of it all – and one that won't always make it onto Christmas cards. And whatever the religious people say – the Saviour of the world has arrived.

OPENING UP

> What does the nativity story mean to you? How do you imagine it? Do you find it difficult to separate the real story from the children's story?

> What do you think are the most important aspects of the nativity story? The baby, the parents, the shepherds, the kings, the star... the donkey? Why?

> Why do you think God chose to send his Son to earth in this way – placed in a manger, no room at the inn and so on...?

> What does it tell us about Jesus that he humbled himself to become a tiny baby – even though he was God?

DIGGING DEEPER

> Is Christmas a positive time for you and your family? Why or why not?

> What do you think people focus on at Christmas today? Do you think they sense there is an important spiritual side to the festival? Do people think Christ is important at Christmas any more?

> What could you change about your celebration of Christmas to give greater recognition to Jesus?

TAKING IT TO THE WORD

➤ **Read** Luke 2:1–20.

> ➤ Why do you think God chose an unmarried woman to give birth to Jesus? How do you think onlookers might have felt about her bump?

> ➤ Why do you think God didn't arrange for there to be room at the inn?!

> ➤ What is the significance of shepherds (and kings, see Matthew 2) coming to visit Jesus? What might their presence at his side suggest or illustrate?

> ➤ Verse 19 says Mary 'treasured up all these things and pondered them in her heart'. What do you think this means?

D17
THEME: Jesus' line
BIBLE: Luke 3

A family business

In recent years, it has become popular for people to look into their family history. The breakdown of the family is both making it more difficult for many people to keep track of their family tree, and feeding a desire to find out where we came from. Who were our great, great grandparents? How did they live? What did they do? It's interesting stuff – because without those people, we wouldn't be here.

The Bible contains a number of family trees, called genealogies. We tend to pass over them, partly because they're little more than lists of names, and partly because those names are so tricky to read! You know the sort of thing: Shabina-habadab was the son of Opadopa-ding-dang-doo... No one wants to be doing the reading in church when that story gets covered.

In fact, these lists are important, because they demonstrate how God's people are part of a line that stretches back thousands and thousands of years. One list, found in Luke 3, is perhaps the most important of all – it traces Jesus' earthly family back all the way through David, Abraham, Noah and Adam (showing the way God's promises to these followers were fulfilled). If we haven't spotted it on our way through the Bible, here it's explained for us backwards: one unbroken family line runs from the fall of humankind through Adam to the redemption of humankind through Jesus. Pretty cool, isn't it?

OPENING UP

➤ How important is your family history to you? How much of it can you draw out on paper, just from the top of your head?

➤ What do you think you've inherited from your family? Looks... mannerisms... ways of doing things?

➤ What do you hope to pass on to any children that you might have?

DIGGING DEEPER

➤ Why do you think there has been a resurgence in people trying to trace their family history?

➤ What is society's view of family right now, as portrayed through the media, people we know etc.? Are you aware of any changes in the importance or role of family?

➤ What do you think a strong family looks like? What might be the positive and negative aspects of living in this kind of family?

TAKING IT TO THE WORD

➤ **Read** Luke 3:21–38.

➤ Why is this relevant if Jesus was a virgin birth to Mary, and therefore Joseph wasn't his real father?

➤ Whose are the names that you recognize on this list? What do you think is significant about their part in Jesus' earthly family?

➤ Why do you think Jesus waited until he was 30 before beginning his ministry on earth?

D18
THEME: Discipleship
BIBLE: Luke 5

Worth following

We all follow something or someone. It's just a question of how closely we do it.

Most people follow a sports team – sometimes religiously closely. But when things aren't going so well, and the team isn't performing on the pitch or court, we're often quick to turn our backs on them. For many people, how closely you follow your team is directly related to how well they're doing.

We also tend to follow other people. Charismatic leaders in our family, community, friendship group or church have more influence over us than we'd sometimes like to admit. Add into that mix our favourite music and movie stars, our choices of brands and media channels, and any other heroes, and you'll see that we're all following a mass of influences.

But how much? How committed are we to the things we follow? If our favourite coffee shop puts its prices up, do we keep drinking there or move to the new place that's just opened across the street? If our favourite celebrity makes a racist outburst on live television, do they remain our favourite, or do we turn against them?

Jesus didn't do anything like that, but he did frequently do and say things that would have blown his followers' minds. He didn't act in the way they expected; he asked them to do things that were way out of their comfort zones. By today's standards, it seems strange that Jesus' disciples never turned around and told him 'no', or never simply walked off and returned to their fishing boats.

There was something about Jesus that meant he was worth following. So much so, that when he called his disciples, they literally stopped in the middle of what they were doing, and physically walked after him. Everything they had known and worked towards for their entire lives, they just dropped, there and then. Following Jesus was irresistible to them.

OPENING UP

➤ What are some of the teams, people, brands and other things that you follow?

➤ How important are these to you? Which is the most important? Why?

➤ Can you think of anyone who follows something as devotedly as Jesus' disciples followed him?

DIGGING DEEPER

➤ Why do you think Jesus selected close followers to live and work alongside him?

➤ Why do you think the twelve disciples were prepared to completely change their lives in this way?

➤ Do you think Jesus' call to us today is exactly the same, or different somehow? Explain your answer.

➤ Do you think you could be completely devoted to following something or someone like they were? Be honest! Could you follow Jesus in this way?

TAKING IT TO THE WORD

➤ **Read** Luke 5:1–11.

➤ Why do you think Jesus performed a miracle on the boat before calling Simon, James and John?

➤ What does he mean in verse 10 by 'from now on you will catch men'?

➤ How do you imagine verse 11? What might have been some of the consequences? What would have happened in the fishing community?

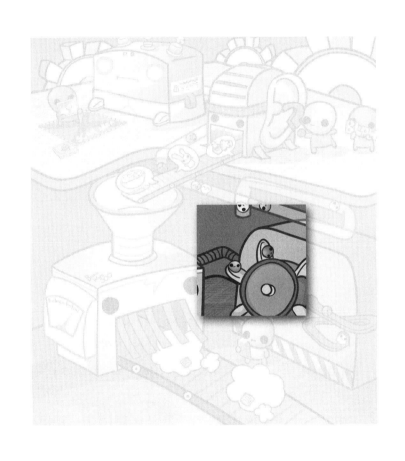

D19

THEME: **Prayer (and forgiveness)**

BIBLE: **Matthew 6**

On earth as it is in heaven

Why do people pray today? Regardless of whether or not they have a faith in God, it's usually for one reason – things are not going well. Subconsciously, every human being knows that he or she does not possess within him/herself the strength to overcome every situation. And deep within all of us, there's a knowledge that there is someone bigger out there who we can cry out to.

So whether your plane is going down, or maybe your exam paper is just full of questions you didn't study for, it's a pretty safe bet that almost without knowing it, you'll allow a few words to leap heavenwards from your lips. 'Please, God... help me...' is probably the phrase that God hears most often.

As a real person, Jesus knew this about humans. But since he was also God, he knew that there was so much more to prayer; that there was so much that people were missing out on. That's why Jesus gave some of his most direct teaching on this very subject. Often, he spoke in riddles, questions and stories, but it seems he was so concerned that people got prayer right, that he actually provided a template – it's almost the exact opposite to his usual style of education.

Jesus' prayer doesn't just ask God for help, it also appreciates God for what he has already done, and perhaps most importantly, focuses heavily on forgiveness. He doesn't just tell us to ask for forgiveness, however – he includes a promise in the prayer that we'll also forgive others. Then, as he explains the prayer, he actually tells his followers that unless they forgive each other, God won't forgive them!

Jesus' prayer is much broader than the ones we usually come up with. It doesn't just talk to God as if he's a big Santa Claus in the sky, waiting to be asked for gifts – instead it is designed to build and grow a real relationship between a human being and God.

OPENING UP

➤ How easy or difficult do you find it to pray? When do you pray? How?

➤ What do you tend to pray about? What don't you pray about?

➤ Have you ever seen a prayer answered? What happened?

DIGGING DEEPER

➤ How easy or difficult do you find it to forgive people?

➤ What's easy to forgive? What is perhaps more difficult?

➤ What do you think is the relationship between our forgiveness of others, and God's forgiveness of us?

➤ Why do you think it's so important to God that we forgive one another?

TAKING IT TO THE WORD

➤ **Read** Matthew 6:5–15.

➤ Why does Jesus call the men described in verse 5 'hypocrites'?

➤ Why should we pray in secret? Does this mean prayer meetings are bad?

➤ If our Father knows what we need before we ask him (verse 8), why bother?

➤ Why should we pray that God's will is done on earth as it is in heaven? What does this mean?

➤ What do verses 14–15 tell us about forgiveness? Do you find this shocking? Do you need to do anything as a result?

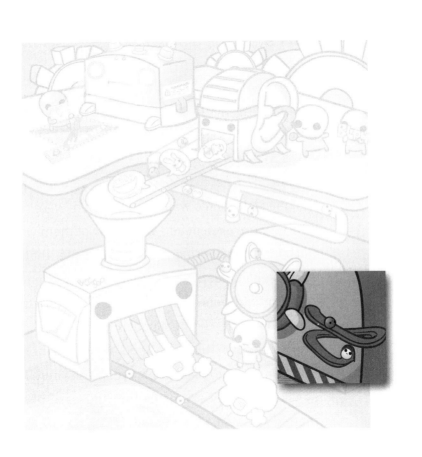

D20
THEME: **Healing**
BIBLE: **Mark 8**

A strange healing

One of Jesus' many roles as a minister (alongside shepherding his flock, teaching, challenging injustice and more) was that of healer. There are several occasions we know about, and many that we don't know the details of, where Jesus demonstrated his power by making sick people well. Some of them were really sick – three were even dead – and many of them were blind. Perhaps, considering Jesus' message that he had come to help people 'see', that's no coincidence.

You might think that Jesus would have a tried-and-tested formula for healing blind people, but in fact, every time he does it, he does it a different way. Sometimes he touches their eyes; elsewhere he simply speaks and they are healed. In the case of the blind man of Bethsaida, not only does he use the most bizarre method, he almost seems to need two chances to get it right.

This short encounter – described in just a few verses – is packed with incident. Jesus spits on his hands, and puts them on the man's eyes. However, he has to do it twice before it works. The man's sight is restored, though – further proof that God is working powerfully among the people again.

OPENING UP

➤ Do you believe God heals today? Why or why not?

➤ What do you know about healing – what have been your experiences of it?

➤ Why do you think healing works sometimes, but not always?

DIGGING DEEPER

➤ Why do you think Jesus heals different people in different ways? Why not just have a one-size-fits-all method?

➤ What does this tell us about God and his character?

➤ How might this influence our approach to healing today? How might it influence our approach to worship, prayer and other aspects of the Christian life?

TAKING IT TO THE WORD

➤ **Read** Mark 8:22–26.

➤ What do we learn about Jesus' character in these verses (particularly verses 23 and 26)?

➤ Is Jesus making a point by healing the man in two stages? What might it be?

➤ Why do you think Jesus told him not to go back into the village?

D21

THEME: **Jesus' death and resurrection**

BIBLE: **John 19 – 20**

The main event

Easter. A time of chocolate eggs, sweet little bunnies, and bloody torture. Whatever the marketing men might have made it, the Easter weekend commemorates humanity's darkest hour.

God came to earth in human form, and never made a single mistake. He was absolutely perfect, and his example led thousands to follow him. He healed the sick, preached good news to the poor, and taught the wisest words ever spoken.

So what did humankind do? They trapped him, rushed him through an unfair trial, and put him to death in the most horrific way. Crucifixion was one of the most terrible forms of capital punishment ever devised – men were nailed to wooden crosses, and literally hung from the nails in their wrists and feet. Every breath was agony – the sufferers eventually died when they could no longer raise their lungs to take a breath.

And so, in this torturous way, Jesus died. But as we all know, that wasn't the end of the story. Easter also commemorates the greatest moment in human history – just two days after the great low point.

Jesus, true to his promise, rose from the dead. He defeated death, and so opened up the way between humankind and God. The chasm that existed between the two since the fall of Adam has been bridged, and now we can choose to enjoy the results of Jesus' victory.

OPENING UP

➤ What do you think would happen if Jesus came to earth today? Would we be more understanding than the people in his time? Why or why not?

➤ If Jesus came to the modern world, do you think humankind would end up killing him? Explain your answer.

➤ How do you think people who had seen Jesus die would have reacted to seeing him walking around three days later? How would you have reacted?

DIGGING DEEPER

➤ How would Christianity be different if Jesus hadn't risen from the dead?

➤ Why do you think Jesus had to die? Why not just get God to forgive everyone? And why die in this terrible way?

➤ How do you feel about the agony that Jesus went through on the cross? What does it mean to you that he did this for you personally?

➤ Why is it important that Jesus rose again?

TAKING IT TO THE WORD

➤ **Read** John 19:16 – 20:9.

➤ Why do you think it's important that Old Testament prophecies were fulfilled (see 19:24, 36–37)? What does 'all was now completed' (verse 28) mean?

➤ What do you think is the importance of the 'garden' at the place where Jesus had been crucified? Where else is there a garden in the Bible? How might these two gardens be related?

➤ How do you think Peter and John (the other disciple mentioned) would have felt when they saw that Jesus' tomb was empty?

D22

THEME: **The Holy Spirit**

BIBLE: **Acts 2**

Getting into the Spirit

Jesus has just left the earth, and doing so must have left quite a vacuum. Now his followers are left with the hard task of taking his message out far and wide. Jesus lit the spark – but now it's up to them to start a fire.

After the eleven remaining followers have replaced the treacherous Judas with a new disciple, Matthias, the very next thing we read about is the coming of the Holy Spirit. On the day of Pentecost, the twelve – now known as 'apostles', having graduated from being disciples – are all gathered together when something extraordinary happens.

Heaven opens, and tongues of fire descend. It sounds like something out of a science-fiction movie. The apostles are struck full in the face by the power of God, and they physically react – quite bizarrely, they begin to speak in other languages; languages that none of them have ever spoken before.

The scene draws a crowd, many of whom are speakers of the languages that the apostles are using. They are shocked by what they hear. 'How is this possible?'

they ask each other. 'What does this mean?' The words are clear, but the meaning behind them is not.

From this point on, the apostles grow in faith and in number, and begin to travel the country, and then the earth, watching the church ignite into life as they go. They may no longer have Jesus standing beside them, but in the Spirit they have one just as powerful.

OPENING UP

➤ What do you know/think/feel about the Holy Spirit? Do you find him a comfortable subject? Why or why not?

➤ Do you believe the Holy Spirit is still involved in the world and in our lives today? If so, how? If not, why not?

➤ Why do you think God would send his Spirit to live in and among us? What do you think the purpose and role of the Spirit is?

DIGGING DEEPER

➤ Why do you think the Spirit causes the apostles to speak in different languages?

➤ Do you believe people can speak in tongues today? What might be the purpose of this? (Look at 1 Corinthians 14 for more on this.)

TAKING IT TO THE WORD

➤ **Read** Acts 2:1–13.

> ➤ Why do you think the Spirit makes such an incredible entrance? Why is it important that this extraordinary scene takes place *after* Jesus makes his exit?
>
> ➤ Verse 4 talks about the Spirit as an 'enabler'. What does this tell us about him? What else do we learn about him?
>
> ➤ What do you find interesting about the presence of the 'God-fearing Jews from every nation under heaven' (verse 5)?
>
> ➤ What is the answer to the question posed in verse 12?
>
> ➤ Why do people suggest that those affected by the Spirit must be drunk? How do people try to explain away the Spirit's work today?

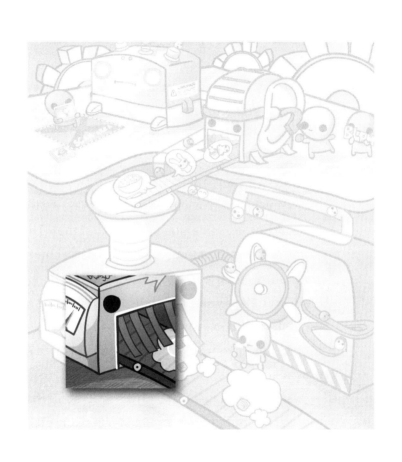

D23
THEME: **Church**
BIBLE: **Acts 4**

More than bells and steeples

Christmas and Easter apart, church is not everyone's favourite place to be. However, if today's church was more like the original ones, perhaps it might be a different story.

In Acts 4 we read about a prayer meeting where the room literally shook with the power of God when everyone said 'Amen'. Imagine being part of that! That sort of experience was not unusual for the early church, which was full of such passionate, committed people that it grew completely out of hand. Two thousand years on, the faith has nearly two billion followers – it's unlikely that without people like the apostles, it would ever have grown so large.

It's fair to suggest that there was something about the early church that made it ripe for growth. Yes, Jesus had only just left the earth, and had left some talented leaders behind him, but there was something else about the church that made it irresistibly attractive to people.

The members of the church had an amazing attitude to possessions. They lived as if they didn't really own anything – sharing everything with one another. Because of this generous approach, no one went hungry. Not only that, the Bible tells us that 'the Lord added to their number daily those who were being saved.' Is it too shocking to suggest that if today's church took a similar approach to money and 'stuff', it might see the same thing happening?

OPENING UP

➤ What is church? Is it people, or buildings, or both?

➤ Why do you think it's important for groups of Christians to gather together? What benefit might doing so have? Are there any negative results?

➤ Do you think Christians are still prepared to share everything they have with one another? Why or why not?

➤ Do you think this kind of living is more radical today than it would have been 2,000 years ago? Why or why not?

➤ What kind of impact do you think the church would make today if people really did take this attitude to money?

DIGGING DEEPER

➤ What do you think the point of church is?

➤ How do you feel about church? Do you find it easy or difficult to go along?

➤ Do you feel 'at home' in church? Explain your answer.

➤ How important do you think your local church is to the community around it?

TAKING IT TO THE WORD

➤ **Read** Acts 4:23–37.

➤ How much of what you see in these verses goes on in churches today?

➤ What signs do we have in this passage (and in Acts 2:42–47) that these people were getting it right, that God was pleased with them?

➤ What seem to be the focuses of the church described here?

➤ How might we need to change our own churches to get back to the original blueprint? What barriers might there be to doing so?

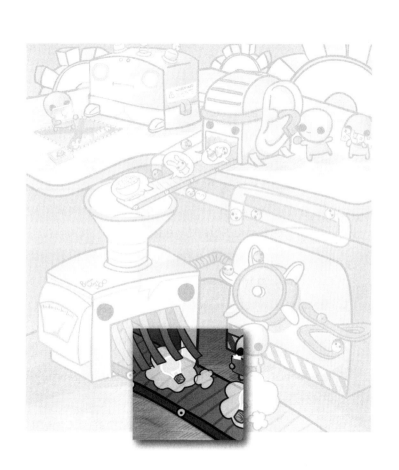

D24

THEME: **Paul**

BIBLE: **Philippians 1**

An unlikely hero

The great hero of the New Testament (Jesus apart!) was a strange-looking man who spent much of his life trying to bring Christianity down before it had begun. Paul's first appearance in the Bible comes as he over- sees the killing of Stephen, one of the church's leading lights. Yet a short time after that, everything in Paul's life got turned on its head.

Imagine being so sure of something that you were willing to kill – and then realizing you'd got it all com- pletely wrong. That's what happened to Paul – Jesus appeared to him and demanded that he turn his life around. As he stumbled away from that encounter, temporarily blinded by God's light, he must have felt foolish and ashamed.

Paul didn't hide away in embarrassment, however. Almost instantly, he re-channelled all of his energy towards making the name of Jesus known throughout the earth. Whereas once he'd been the church's biggest enemy, now he resolved to become its greatest weapon.

Paul racked up more stamps in his passport than a

touring pop star, as he took the gospel message far and wide. He wrote great chunks of the New Testament, despite having to spend years of his life in prison for preaching an illegal and radical message. He oversaw tremendous growth in the church, and handled the responsibility of correcting churches that misunderstood.

Paul is perhaps the greatest example of the fact that, with God's help, anyone can turn their life around. Through his story, we learn that God can use anyone, no matter what they've done wrong.

OPENING UP

➤ How do you think Paul must have felt when he realized he'd got it all wrong about Jesus?

➤ Why do you think God was prepared to make such great use of Paul, when he had overseen the killing of Stephen?

➤ What do we learn about God from Paul's story?

➤ Why do you think Paul was so sure of what he was doing? After all, he'd seemed pretty sure when he was persecuting the Christians...

DIGGING DEEPER

➤ How have you seen God use you in the lives of others?

➤ Do you believe God can use you as much as he used Paul? Why or why not?

➤ What stories have you heard of people turning their lives around with God's help? What happened?

TAKING IT TO THE WORD

➤ **Read** Philippians 1.

> ➤ Why do you think Paul wrote letters like these?
>
> ➤ What do you think it would have meant for the church in Philippi to hear these words of love from Paul (verses 3–8)? What do you think the reaction would have been in the church when a letter from Paul arrived?
>
> ➤ What do you learn about Paul's character from his attitude to his prison sentence? How could we be more like this?
>
> ➤ What is Paul's attitude to his mission?
>
> ➤ Why do you think Paul has such love for the church?

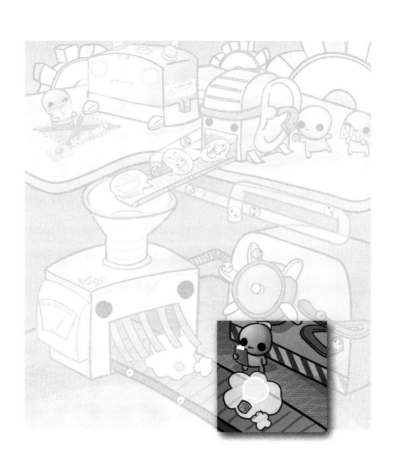

D25

THEME: ## Life after death
BIBLE: ## Revelation 21

Something to look forward to

The Bible is a very long book. So it's quite a relief to find that on the final pages, there's a very happy ending in store. The Book of Revelation contains John's prophetic vision of heaven – the place where God dwells, and where humankind and God will finally come together for eternity. It's the end of this chapter of God's story – and we're still living in a time before it happens.

The amazing thing here is that we have a picture of God himself coming down to be with humankind. The Bible starts with humans hiding from God and God punishing them, and finishes with God making himself at home in a renewed heaven and earth where all evil is disposed of. We can enjoy him and his presence forever in new bodies fitted for the exploration of a glorious universe – a fantastic future that makes sci-fi predictions seem tame by comparison.

This, then, is the part of the Bible that hasn't yet happened – it's our future. Revelation promises that, thanks to Jesus, the future we can look forward to is glorious on every level. We can only imagine what it is going to look like, but we do know that it will be a place without 'death, or mourning, or crying, or pain'.

Heaven is described as a place where there is no night – where there is no need for a sun or moon because the glory of God lights it up so magnificently. It sounds perfect, and of course it is. But there's a sting in the tail – through Jesus, this is what is possible for everyone when they die, but it isn't the only afterlife that Revelation describes.

There's also a place reserved for 'the cowardly, the unbelieving and the vile', which is only described as a fiery lake of burning sulphur. If these were two holiday destinations, the average tourist wouldn't spend long deciding between them. Yet it seems from Revelation that this choice is put before us all – eternity in God's paradise, or a 'second death' which separates us from him forever.

Thanks to free will, God has placed the decision in our own hands. If we choose to grasp it, the end of our story can be happy. In fact, it's only the beginning...

OPENING UP

➤ What do you think happens after we die?

➤ What do you imagine heaven looks and feels like?

➤ Does the idea of living forever excite, confuse or concern you? Explain your answer.

DIGGING DEEPER

➤ What do you think hell is? What do you imagine from that word?

➤ What worries or concerns do you have about death and the afterlife?

➤ Do you think you're headed for heaven or hell? Explain your answer.

TAKING IT TO THE WORD

➤ **Read** Revelation 21:1–14, 22–27.

➤ Why do you think there needs to be a new heaven and a new earth? What's wrong with the old ones?

➤ What do you think is meant by the term 'second death' (verse 8)?

➤ Why do you think the tribes of Israel and the apostles are mentioned (verses 12–14)? How do these verses help to draw the whole story of the Bible together?

➤ What does it mean to have your name written in the Lamb's book of life (verse 27)?

Index

Abilities, 55, 92–94
Acceptance, 110
Addiction, 36, 86, 118, 152, 162
Adultery, 32, 100
Advertising, 68–69
Age, 54–55
Alcohol, 55, 67, 102, 162
Anger, 46, 240, 269
Apartheid, 190
Atheism, 200
Authority, 56

Breaking Up, 122

Capital Punishment, 179, 192, 194, 288
Career, 27, 46, 150, 158, 168, 170, 174, 190
Celebration, 170, 274
Charity, 25, 159, 172–173, 178, 186–187
Cheating, 33, 36, 114–116, 142–143
Church, 21, 46, 55, 68–69, 75, 78, 84–85, 105–106, 124, 151, 181, 199, 276, 293, 296–298, 300–302
Computer Games, 132–133
Conviction, 42–43
Courage, 30, 42–43
Creation, 39, 202, 210, 212–213, 217

Death, 18, 30, 38, 155, 177, 193–194, 204–205, 229, 240, 254, 288–289, 304–306
Dieting, 130–131, 136–137, 168
Disability, 196, 237

Divorce, 33, 36–37, 75, 134–135
Drugs, 19, 66–67, 102–103, 149

Eating Disorders, 130, 136
Education, 67, 206–207, 283
Emotion, 19, 22–23, 35
Environment, 183, 188
Equality, 190
Ethics, 74, 186
Evolution, 212–213

Fairness, 138, 140
Faith, 19, 26–27, 31, 191, 200, 202, 205, 229, 248–249, 257, 282, 293, 296
Fashion, 60–61, 72, 84, 130–131
Forgiveness, 46–48, 282–284
Friendship, 74, 98, 103, 136, 144, 146, 166–167, 238, 278

Generosity, 24–25, 176–177, 186
Giving Thanks, 188
God's People, 220–222, 224, 228–230, 242, 265, 269, 276
Gossip, 104, 142–143
Graffiti, 72–73

Healing, 286–287
Holy Spirit, 124–125, 266, 292–293
Homosexuality, 74, 104
Hoodies, 61
Hope, 26–28, 39, 73, 83, 130, 134, 153, 208, 211, 260–261, 277
Hypocrisy, 58–59

Integrity, 96–97
Internet Pornography, 36–37

Jealousy, 126–127

Law, 57, 71, 187, 190, 228–230, 256
Laziness, 78–79
Lies, 142–143
Life After Death, 304

Marriage, 32–33, 36, 40, 45–46, 98,
    135, 150–151
Maturity, 54, 152
Money, 24–25, 40, 77, 84, 94, 96–97,
    108–109, 131, 152–153, 166,
    172–173, 176–178, 189, 206, 236,
    297
Music Piracy, 76

National Rivalry, 34
Natural Disasters, 38–39, 42, 249
Near Death Experience, 30

Parents, 20, 42, 86, 90–91, 98,
    102–103, 108, 115, 132–134,
    144–145, 151, 156–157, 209, 274
Peer Pressure, 102–103
Persecution, 112, 221
Perseverance, 26, 43, 196–198
Political Protest, 52
Pornography, 37, 86–87, 180
Possessions, 64–65, 94, 187
Poverty, 192, 237
Power, 125, 162, 179, 182–184, 202,
    232–233, 240, 244, 246, 261, 286,
    292, 296
Prayer, 28, 30–31, 87, 104, 124,
    156–157, 241, 282–284, 287, 296
Punishment, 36, 52, 165, 268

Racism, 20–21, 34, 164–165, 278
Relationships, 22, 27, 33, 36, 41, 71,
    122–123, 135, 151, 157, 166
Religion, 35, 180–181, 191, 200–201
Reputation, 62–63, 78, 110, 139,
    174–175
Rescue, 26, 54, 99, 205, 220, 224–225
Revenge, 50–51
Rules, 70–71, 74, 123, 125, 228–229

Sabbath, The, 74, 80, 84–85
Second Chances, 178–179
Self Image, 131, 137, 168
Sexual Guilt, 98
Sexuality, 74
Sin, 39, 45, 87, 131, 194, 216–217, 230
Slavery, 71, 221, 224–226, 228, 243,
    265
Sport, 27, 35, 60, 71, 77, 85, 118, 167,
    188, 278
Star Wars, 64–65, 170, 213
Stealing, 108–109

Talents, 92–94, 246, 253
Television, 18, 22, 27, 118–119, 148,
    150, 162, 166, 180, 278
Text Messages, 11, 52, 156–157
Tsunami, 38–39, 42

Unrequited Love, 82

Virginity, 44–45, 99

War, 24, 34, 52–53, 56, 192–193
Wisdom, 43, 135, 244, 256–257, 273
Worship, 124–125, 189, 240, 242, 249,
    252–253, 287

Youth, 54

Youthwork the partnership
– The Initiatives

Youthwork the partnership

ALOVE (The Salvation Army for a new generation), Oasis, Spring Harvest, Youth for Christ and Youthwork magazine are working together to equip and resource the church for effective youthwork and ministry.

The partnership exists to offer support, encouragement and ideas for busy youth workers including:

Youthwork the conference

Youthwork the conference is a weekend event designed for church-based volunteer youth workers, with specific streams for younger leaders and salaried youth workers. Youthwork the conference has been designed to give training and support by offering encouragement, ideas and resources to busy youth workers. There is also an additional early day conference specifically for full time youth workers.

The conference includes: Main plenary sessions with teaching, worship, prayer, reflection and encouragement plus many practical and skills based seminars covering a wide range of youthwork issues. There is also opportunities to network with others; space to reflect and pray, and access to a large range of youth ministry specialist agencies via an extensive exhibition and resource area.

Youthwork the conference takes place each November. Visit www.youthwork.co.uk/conference or call 0870 060 3327 for more information.

Youthwork the conference is administrated by Spring Harvest.

Youthwork magazine

Since 1992, Youthwork magazine has been the magazine of choice for youth workers across the UK. Every issue is packed with resources, information and opinion, providing youth workers with all the latest news on youth ministry and youth culture. Each month there are book, cd and resource reviews, challenging and inspiring articles, Jobsearch, must-see websites, and a pull-out section packed with ready-to-use curriculum resources including drama, discussion triggers, and ways to use music and film with your group. With all this and more jammed into every issue, it's no surprise that so many youth workers consider Youthwork magazine essential reading.

On sale in most Christian bookshops. Visit www.youthwork.co.uk/magazine or call 01892 652364 for more information or to subscribe.

Youthwork magazine is published by CCP Limited.

Youthwork the resources

A series of books to help youth workers in their youth-work and ministry, in three categories. 'Developing Practice' titles are designed for all those engaged in youthwork and ministry. They are inspirational and practical without being overtly theoretical. 'Challenging Thinking' titles are designed for those who are serious about youthwork and ministry. They are sometimes controversial, always challenging, but never dogmatic. 'Resourcing Ministry' titles provide busy youth workers with tried and tested ideas and curriculum to use with their young people.

Visit www.youthwork.co.uk/resources or call 01825 769111 for more information.

Youthwork the resources are published by Spring Harvest Publishing.

Youthwork the training

WHAT EVERY VOLUNTEER YOUTH WORKER SHOULD KNOW

A training course for busy 'extra timers' who need to know the basics – and fast! This innovative course pro-vides a foundation of knowledge, tips and resources in an accessible and practical format. The course is made up of 9 two-hour sessions which may be delivered in a variety of ways to fit needs and lifestyle! You can choose when and where you do the sessions.

Participation includes a free resource book and 100 ready-to-use ideas. The course is endorsed by a broad spectrum of Christian denominations and networks.

Visit www.youthwork.co.uk/training/volunteerscourse or call 0207 450 9044 for more information.

'What Every Volunteer Youthworker Should Know' is managed and delivered by Oasis.

The Art of Connecting

A resource to equip you and your youth group to see lives changed...forever! The vision behind 'The Art of Connecting' is the realisation that people communicate most naturally when they are exploring their own stories together. The course aims to empower people to share their faith through story – making connections between their story, their friends' stories and God's story.

'The Art of Connecting' Leaders Guide and 'My Story' Journal are available, as are regional training days for youth leaders and young people.

Visit www.youthwork.co.uk/training/aoc or call 0121 550 8055 for more information.

'The Art of Connecting' is developed and delivered by Youth for Christ.

Youthwork online

www.youthwork.co.uk features a dynamic home page updated weekly with the latest information, news analysis and views on youthwork and youth culture – all things that will be of interest to all those working with young people. It's also the place to find out about the partnership and how we can support you, including more details on the conference, magazine, training courses, and resources, and access to the Youthwork online directory.

At www.youthwork.co.uk/community there is a range of online discussion forums with discussions on youth ministry issues, plus forums to share and resources with other youth workers from across the country.

Visit www.youthwork.co.uk for more information.

Youthwork online is owned by CCP Limited and developed by all the partners.

Youthwork the partnership
– The Partners

OASIS

Oasis develops effective ways of transforming the lives of the poor and marginalised and whole communities in the UK and around the world. We help churches and individuals do the same.

Drawing on 20 years experience of pioneering mission, education and youth work initiatives; Oasis provides opportunities for young people to participate in life changing UK and Global mission on both a short and long term basis and equips youth workers with innovative resources and training including the 'What Every Volunteer Youth Worker Should Know' course & the JNC-qualifying Oasis Youth Work and Ministry Degree.

Oasis also enables youth workers and church volunteers to support young people's personal, social and health education in their local schools through training associate educators in Sex and Relationships Education and Mentoring as well as tackling social exclusion among young people head on through the delivery of one to one transition work, mentoring and supported housing programmes.

To find out more:

Visit: www.oasistrust.org

Email: enquiries@oasistrust.org

Phone: 0207 450 9000

Write to: Oasis, The Oasis Centre, 115 Southwark Bridge Road, London,

SE1 0AX, England.

ALOVE

The Salvation Army for a new generation

ALOVE is The Salvation Army for a new generation. ALOVE is calling a generation to dynamic faith, radical lifestyle, adventurous mission and a fight for justice.

ALOVE provides young people and young adults with ongoing opportunities to engage in culturally engaging worship, cell and small group discipleship, innovative mission and world changing social action.

ALOVE runs training programmes to develop leaders and missionaries for the 21st century. ALOVE is also pioneering new expressions of church, youth work and social inclusion in communities around the United Kingdom and Ireland.

To find out more about ALOVE:

Visit: www.salvationarmy.org.uk/ALOVE

Email: ALOVE@salvationarmy.org.uk

Phone: 0208 288 1202

Write to: ALOVE UK, The Salvation Army, 21 Crown Lane, Morden, Surrey, SM4 5BY, England.

SPRING HARVEST

Spring Harvest's vision is to 'equip the Church for action'. Through a range of events, conferences, courses and resources we enable Christians to impact their local communities and the wider world.

Spring Harvest is probably best known for Main Event, held every Easter, which attracts over 55,000 people of all ages. Over 10,000 of those attending are young people. The Main Event also includes specific streams which cater for over 2,000 students. Alongside the teaching programme, Spring Harvest provide a range of resources for young people and those involved in youth ministry.

Through our sister company – Spring Harvest Holidays – we offer quality holidays at our four-star holiday park in the Vendee, France. These inspirational holidays cater for people of all ages in a safe, secure and relaxed environment.

The Spring Harvest range of resources – albums, books and teaching resources – all aim to equip the Church for action.

To find out more about Spring Harvest:

Visit: www.springharvest.org

Email: info@springharvest.org

Phone: 01825 769000

Write to: Spring Harvest, 14 Horsted Square, Uckfield, East Sussex, TN22 1QG, England.

YOUTH FOR CHRIST

Youth for Christ (YFC), one of the most dynamic Christian organisations, are taking good news relevantly to every young person in Britain. They help tackle the big issues facing young people today. They're going out on the streets, into schools, communities and young offenders institutes and have changed the lives of countless people throughout the UK.

Their staff, trainees and volunteers currently reach over 70,000 young people each week and have over 65 centres in locations throughout the UK. They also provide creative arts and sports mission teams, a network of registered groups and a strong emphasis on 'three-story' evangelism. YFC International works in 120 nations.

To find out more about YFC:

Visit: www.yfc.co.uk

Email: churchresource@yfc.co.uk

Phone: 0121 550 8055

Write to: YFC, PO Box 5254, Halesowen, West Midlands B63 3DG, England.

YOUTHWORK MAGAZINE

Youthwork magazine is Britain's most widely read magazine resource for Christian youth workers. Through articles, ready-to-use resources, reviews, youthwork and cultural news and analysis, and much more, Youthwork magazine provides ideas, resources and guidance to help you in your work with young people.

Youthwork magazine is published monthly by CCP Limited, which is part of the Premier Media Group, who also publish Christianity and Christian Marketplace.

To find out more about Youthwork magazine:

Visit: www.youthwork.co.uk

Email: youthwork@premier.org.uk

Phone: 01892 652364

Write to: Youthwork Magazine, CCP Limited, Broadway House, The Broadway, Crowborough, TN6 1HQ, England.

You may also appreciate:

The Art of Connecting

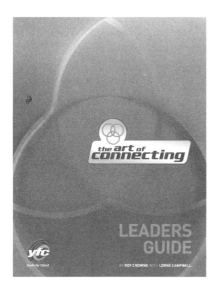

How can we share our faith with those around us?

It starts with us telling our own stories, sharing our hopes, dreams and desires: simple stories of everyday, ordinary lives, shared between friends.

Every person who has done this course has felt released and excited – because it works.

"A key resource for your youth programme." **MIKE PILAVACHI**

ISBN: 978-1-85424-831-2

Available from your local Christian bookshop.

In case of difficulty, please visit our website: www.lionhudson.com